ZEN

Poems, Prayers, Sermons, Anecdotes, Interviews

Lucien Stryk was brought up in Chicago and attended Indiana University, the State University of Iowa and, in Europe, the Sorbonne and University of London. He has published three books of poetry, *Taproot*, *The Trespasser*, and *Notes for a Guidebook*, as well as prose and verse in over fifty periodicals and anthologies, ranging from *The Listener* (London) and the *Saturday Review* to university quarterlies. In 1963 he shared a first prize in the *Chicago Daily News*' New "Chicago" Poem Competition and in 1964 won *Voices*' annual Isaac Rosenbaum Poetry Award. He has held a Fulbright Lectureship in Iran and has twice been a Visiting Lecturer in Japan. He has taught at writers' conferences and has given poetry readings at many colleges and universities, including the University of Chicago, Cornell University, and Wayne State University. At present he teaches Creative Writing and Oriental Literature at Northern Illinois University.

Takashi Ikemoto, born and educated in Japan, is Professor of English at Yamaguchi University. He is a contributor to magazines, both in Japan and in the United States. Seeking to share his profound interest in Zen with English-speaking readers, he has collaborated with Lucien Stryk in many articles. Among the magazines to which he has contributed are *Orient/West*, the *Chicago Review*, *Imagi* (an American poetry magazine), *Vou* (a Japanese avant-garde poetry magazine), *Young East*, and *New Directions Annual*.

ZEN

Poems
Prayers
Sermons
Anecdotes
Interviews

SELECTED AND TRANSLATED
BY LUCIEN STRYK
AND TAKASHI IKEMOTO

Anchor Books
Doubleday & Company, Inc.
Garden City, New York, 1965

Some of this material previously has been published in *Chicago Review, Orient/West, Tri-Quarterly,* and *Young East.*

It gives us great pleasure to acknowledge a real debt, and deep gratitude, to Mrs. Bonnie R. Crown and Miss Susan Conheim of the Asia Society's Asian Literature Program for encouragement and help.

Lucien Stryk is indebted to the Asia Society for a grant that made possible a period of research into Asian literature and language study at Yale University. He also wishes to acknowledge the help given him by the University of Chicago, which awarded him a Ford Foundation Faculty Fellowship to pursue Indic studies related to the rise of Buddhism.

For the listener, who listens in the snow,
And, nothing himself, beholds
Nothing that is not there and the nothing that is.

WALLACE STEVENS, "The Snow Man"

CONTENTS

CONTENTS

INTRODUCTION

In this age of scientism and materialism, people throughout the world are plagued by unrest and self-alienation; daily they stray from themselves, living for nothing but ephemeral pleasures. The Zennist is the opposite of those people: he abides serenely in the here and now, and is above joy and grief, life and death. It is not that he is without worries and afflictions, but, seeing them with his awakened eye, he is enslaved by none of them. He is a man of complete freedom.

In Japan, Zen, or the Way of *satori* ("awakening"), has been maintained in its traditional integrity. Zennist monks are guided by a master, or *shike*; training is conducted in a hall of a Zen temple, or *sodo*, specially reserved for that purpose. There, every day, the monks engage in *zazen*, which is to sit cross-legged in Zen contemplation. Also, in individual visits (*dokusan*), they offer their responses to Zen questions (*koan*), which the master has previously posed. One such koan might be Joshu's *Mu* ("Nothingness").

Disciplinary procedures vary somewhat from sect to sect, and features attributable to the personalities of the masters may cause some variations in practice. Guidance is often unique and rigorous—a blow from the master's staff, for example, as well as the "give and take" on the koan, may be used to advance the monk's understanding of Zen, and bring him closer to attaining satori. Training need not be conducted specifically in the sodo, and the title of shike may be applied to a qualified lay master who lives outside a temple.

There were ninety-one sodo in Japan in the beginning of 1961, with presumably not less than ninety-one shike. The number now, four years later, is probably much the same. The number of monks residing in these sodo is not available, but cannot be high. Laymen, too, are allowed to participate in both zazen and dokusan, and even in the special assemblies, such as the austere eight-day assembly which begins on the first of December in commemoration of the Buddha's satori under the bo tree, laymen participate.

There are three Zen sects in Japan: Soto, Rinzai, and Obaku. Of the ninety-one sodo, fifty-three belong to the Soto, thirty-six to the Rinzai, and two to the Obaku sect. The Soto and Rinzai sects differ from one another in outlook and discipline; Obaku, the smallest sect, is identical with Rinzai, save in ritual formalities.

The Soto sect, the largest of the three, and one of the most influential Buddhist sects in Japan, stresses zazen, occasionally utilizing koan to deepen and enliven zazen. To the Soto Zennist zazen is not a means to satori. To engage in zazen is, itself, satori. In a word, zazen is satori, satori zazen. The Soto Zennist is prudent and values consistency of words and deeds. To him, Zen and morality are identical. The relation between disciple and master is like that between knocker and answerer: let the disciple knock and, immediately, the master answers.

The Rinzai sect, on the other hand, stresses koan. The Rinzai follower scrutinizes his koan in zazen to gain satori. He does seek satori. He is rigorous and prizes virile representation of the Zen personality. The master and the disciple have, so to speak, a life-and-death fight: they exchange Zen cries, and the disciple may even deal a blow at the master. The Rinzai Zennist is represented as resembling a stern, majestic general.

Soto and Rinzai are thus marked by contrasting features. The followers of the two sects not infrequently criticize one another, and they are aware of each other's strong and weak points. The Rinzai master, Sogen Omori, suggests in one of his recent books, *Sanzen Nyumon* (A Manual of Zen Practice), that one who wants to practice Zen compare the two sects and choose the one that suits his taste and character. He adds, however, that the vital thing no doubt is to have a good master.

Our list of Zennists is not long, but most of them are prominent masters. The oldest is Eizai (1141–1215), the authentic introducer of the Rinzai sect from China. Dogen (1200–1253), the founder of the Japanese Soto sect, is next. Eizai and Dogen are followed by upholders of Zen throughout its long history, including two priests who live presently in Yamaguchi City. They appear in one or more of the four parts of this anthology.

Zen is practiced only in a section of Japanese society. Many are, therefore, prone to refer to a decline in Zen. They say that Zen is alienated from the life of the masses; the priests stick to the old disciplinary conventions and make no attempt to devise new methods of training; they shut themselves up in their temples, not much concerned about guiding the multitude. But one must not overlook the fact that so-called new inventions in disciplinary method acceptable to the modern citizen may turn out to be more harmful than otherwise; they may lead to the creation of frivolous "instant" Zen, instead of preserving orthodox Zen of "instantaneous" satori (the experience of satori is "instantaneous" and usually comes after a period of hard training). It now appears urgent that the value of traditional discipline be recognized again. The social activities of Zen priests are what they as Mahayanists are expected to engage in, and it is the desire of the supporters of Zen that it become a more vigorous force in contemporary society. But here again a warning will not be out of place; that is, as is justly alleged, that there is no Zen without satori. And satori is a completely subjective experience which no amount of mere social service will enable one to gain. Hence the dictum: first gain satori, and then edify others. I have given the warnings solely to impress on the Western reader the momentousness of orthodox tradition in Zen. Even in Japan, arbitrary deviation from it or capricious dogmatization has characterized the attempts of some lay students of Zen, and given rise to many misunderstandings. Such an unauthentic manipulation, however, has always been a target of masters' criticism and helped the followers of Zen to recognize all the more distinctly the importance of tradition.

However, this is not the whole picture: there are signs of a resurgence of Zen. First, there is at present, comparatively, a large number of prominent lay Zennists. A strong yearning after Zen has for a long time prevailed among some members of the Japanese intelligentsia. These intellectuals may abhor anything smacking of religion and yet be ardent pursuers of Zen. Zen appeals to them as a way of self-realization, devoid of all the supernatural and superstitious. Nantembo (1839–1925), the most influential master in his day, went so far as to declare that he anchored his hope, not on priests, but on laymen. It is to the credit of the Japanese lay followers that eminent Zennists have appeared from among them. The leading contemporary lay Zennists, headed by Dr. Suzuki—some of whom are shike—are contributing toward the Zen revival by training their followers or writing on Zen.

Second, scientific investigations of zazen have been conducted with noticeable results. Professor Kasamatsu of Tokyo University took a measurement of the brain waves of monks in zazen, which revealed that the brain waves of a monk in zazen are of the regular and tranquil α type and resemble those of a man in a light sleep—the exact reverse of a neurotic's agitated brain waves—and yet he remains extremely sensitive to outside stimuli; for instance, he can hear the ashes of an incense stick fall in front of him. This is testimony that zazen can serve not merely as a method of health preservation, but as a cure for neuroses and other diseases. When Professor Kasamatsu published the results of his investigation at a medical meeting in 1959, it was reported by the newspapers and has since aroused popular interest in Zen. Also, Professor Sugi of the Tokyo University of Education, who has always been interested in Zen, has recently made an experiment on "Zazen and Energy Consumption." He discovered that a monk during zazen consumes 20 per cent less than fourteen hundred calories a day, the minimum required to maintain the life of a man at rest. This is sufficient evidence for the fact that zazen saves calories and helps store up stamina.

Third, separate mention may be made of the efforts of two scholars to popularize Zen. Dr. Hasegawa, a physician of Osaka, has for years been propagating what is called "medical Zen." He analyzes zazen from the medical standpoint and finds in it great health benefits. Professor Sato of Kyoto University writing on "psychological Zen," enumerates ten specific examples of benefits that might be derived from zazen, including cure of impatience, strengthened will power, and increased work efficiency.

Fourth, I would like to cite Master Horyu Ishiguro's "prompt-awakening Zen," an ingenious modern type of discipline, of which Professor Sato is an upholder. Under this discipline, Master Ishiguro asserts, one can attain an initial stage of satori in five days. The Ishiguro method is criticized by some masters; nonetheless it is a new device which has created a mild sensation in Zen circles.

Lastly, it must be mentioned that some masters have recently written essays and commentaries of particular relevance to the modern reader: Master Somei Tsuji relates how he, as a layman with a family to support, began undergoing Rinzai discipline, and surmounting hardships, succeeded to the Buddha's Law, finally entering the priesthood; Master Zenkei Shibayama, Abbot of Nanzenji Temple in Kyoto, applies Zen interpretation on the text of a popular epic song.

I have given some of the factors which are responsible for the Zen renascence in modern-day Japan. One example of this phenomenon is the practical interest in Zen shown by the managements of big companies. It is becoming customary to send new employees to Zen temples to undergo training for a fixed period of time. To the employees this means an invigorating moral and spiritual education to which most of them remained indifferent during their school days. They are thus oriented toward responsible fulfillment of their duties. As another example, I should like to cite the case of Yamaguchi University, where I teach English. The university, with more than three thousand students, is located in Yamaguchi City in western Japan. There is at the university a Zen study fraternity with which I and two other faculty members who are keenly interested in Zen are connected. We have just decided to have regular meetings in a Zen temple in the city. Among the other fraternities, there are those of swordsmanship, archery, and tea ceremony, whose members stay in Zen temples for several days to do zazen and practice their arts. This is not to be wondered at, considering the agelong relationship between those arts and Zen. But also the members of the *koto* and the *shakuhachi* music club (the *koto* is normally a musical instrument for females, the *shakuhachi* for males) make a short sojourn in a Zen temple, in the expectation that Zen will help them with their musical attainments. And they seem to leave the temple with a feeling of satisfaction, for they say that, in spite of bodily pain during zazen, they feel refreshed after and can practice their music in a more serene mood. As is well known, the Zen spirit lies at the basis of all the traditional arts in Japan, and student groups practicing any of them have lately begun to receive short-term training in Zen.

There is, fundamentally, no room for words and letters. Dogen wrote: "A Zen follower must do zazen and nothing else. The Way of the Buddha and Patriarchs is none other than zazen." He discouraged his disciples from book learning and writing. The poet Muso (1275–1351) gave a strong warning: "A monk who is given to reading non-Buddhist books and engages in writing is a worldling with a shaven head. He is less than nobody." But Dogen and Muso were both great Buddhist scholars and writers of their day and left writings of first quality. Dogen's *Shobogenzo*, a collection of essays on Zen Buddhism, is one of the most philosophical and stylistically refined works from the Japanese Buddhists' pen. Dogen and Muso were poets as well, and poetry writing has always been a custom with Japanese Zen masters. In China the supporters of Zen were intellectuals, and the Chinese Zen priests were scholars and writers. This tradition has been upheld in Japan.

Masters usually hold that book knowledge is harmful for a beginner but, after he has gone through his training, it will prove of great service to him. It was the natural course that Zennists of a literary turn of mind would, under favorable social conditions, come to put increasing stress upon the role literature should play in the cultivation of Zen. That was the case especially with the priests of the five major Zen temples in Kamakura and Kyoto. Their "five-temple literature" school occupies a conspicuous place in the medieval history of Japanese literature. They asserted that to write poetry is to practice Zen. Keian, for example, was a radical exponent of this theory and declared: "The finer poetry is, the more matured Zen is." This reminds one of the well-known postulate, "Poetry and Zen are of a savor," a postulate which originally prevailed in Chinese Zen communities. The theory advocated by the five-temple literary coteries is erroneous, however. To a poet-monk absorbed in versification, satori will remain a sealed book. Or if he has already gained a measure of satori, it will never mature. The result: his pen, however eloquent, will produce no genuine Zen verse. This is why, in selecting Zen poets for this book, we have excluded poets with no real Zen experience.

Zen literature is an expression of the Inexpressible, and Zen poetry is a typical example. Outsiders will inevitably find something mystical about the Inexpressible in whatever way it is represented. And Zen writers frequently resort to symbols, many of which are mysteriously out of the common. Moreover, stories are told of strange phenomena beginners in Zen are prone to experience—for example, visions of Bodhisattvas (who seek enlightenment so as to be able to save others)—and, of course, of extraordinary experiences of super-common-sense. All this will help promote a mystical interpretation of Zen. In fact, one can, as Lucien Stryk does in his essay in this volume, point to a similarity of expression between Zen and mysticism. But that is all one can do: it does not mean that Zen is mysticism. In the final analysis, Zen has nothing to do with mysticism, especially Christian mysticism. The Westerner's misunderstanding in this respect is gradually being corrected, it appears, but a glance here at Christian mysticism from the Zen point of view will not be out of place.

Christian mysticism may be defined as "the direct union of the human soul with the Divinity through contemplation and love" (*The Catholic Encyclopedia*, Vol. X, 1913, p. 663). The union is alleged to be direct, but it rests nonetheless on a dualism in which man and the personal God stand opposed to one another. Man is helpless and cannot enter into the mystic union unless God wills it. And the Beatific Vision, the greatest possible blessing man can enjoy, is not granted him until after his death. In this life the chosen few are allowed to witness the lesser mystic visions, and common believers must remain content with preparing themselves for the Vision in the next life. Christian poets cannot go beyond giving expression to a sinner's fears, joys, and yearnings. For instance, Traherne, an intensely joyous Christian poet, describes union with God through the divine grace he perceives in created things, but, needless to say, this union is a different thing from a heavenly Vision.

In Zen, union with the Absolute and union with nature are one and the same thing; it is immediate—with no intermediary whatever. There is nothing mystifying about Zen. Zen is clarity itself. It is only that one, misled by dualistic rumination, cannot see the Absolute. To a Zen poet, a thing of beauty or anything in nature *is* the Absolute. Hence his freedom from rationality and his recourse to uncommon symbols. Yet ultimately what he portrays is concrete, not a dreamy fancy or vision.

Kokan Shiren (1278–1364), a leading member of the five-temple literary school and an advocate of grand style poetry, maintains that what constitutes the essence of poetry is the refined and upright mind. This would be a justified proposition as far as secular verse is concerned. But a Zen poet must be more than a man of refined and upright mind: he must be a man of satori. This prerequisite makes for all that characterizes Zen poetry. Its general features may be cited: conciseness, rigor, volitionality, virility, and serenity. As an expression of the inexpressible Absolute, Zen poetry is of course often illogical; it is usually colored and enlivened by what we may call "absolute symbolism." These features mark Zen poems, especially those composed in classical Chinese forms; and most of the pieces of Japanese masters are in that style, the others being *waka* and *haiku*. Zen poetry may take the form of free verse, though Shinkichi Takahashi, a mature lay Zennist, seems to be the only Zen free-verse poet in Japan.

Poems

The poems in this anthology can be divided into three groups, namely, satori poems, death poems, and others on various subjects. A satori poem is composed immediately after one has attained satori and is presented to one's master for approval. It delineates what one's spiritual eye has been opened to. Satori is also called *kensho* ("seeing into one's nature"). In Christian terms it is to see the Beatific Vision not in the next but in this life. Yet, it is not a vision of the Divine Being: such a vision will be rejected as an illusion, an abnormal psychological occurrence. It is, instead, something like a view of things in their eternal aspect: the sight of absolute, primordial Nothingness. The late Dr. Kitaro Nishida, the eminent Zen philosopher, no doubt meant the same thing when he wrote: "From the standpoint of eternal Suchness, we see true God where God is not." There are a great number of satori poems capable of galvanizing aspirants into Zen vitality. Death poems are penned or dictated by Zennists right before death, written as the author looks back on his life and states his frame of mind at the inevitable hour.

Our translation of Zen poetry is an attempt to reproduce the Zen spirit in the original pieces. They are not translated literally because we wanted to avoid producing unpoetic versions.

Prayers

A number of Zen prayers are extant, out of which we have chosen two to show what kind of vows Zen priests take. A Zen prayer is different from a Christian prayer. The latter is usually a petition, adoration, thanksgiving, or contrition addressed to God. The Zennist's prayer is also addressed to the Buddha and the Patriarchs, but is not a petition; it is a Mahayana Buddhist's determination to attain satori and save others.

Sermons

Zen sermons usually treat the questions: "What is Zen, and satori?" and "How can one attain it?" Zen sermons differ from those of most religions in that they do not just expound doctrines. The reader of Zen sermons is not expected to memorize meaningful expressions but to gain immediate satori or to advance a step closer to it. In Zen, belief is not the final thing, though belief in one's own Buddhahood is a vital prerequisite to the practice of Zen. The Zen view is that Truth is beyond verbalization. Yet this fact can best be proclaimed by means of language; hence the masters' readiness to make use of it. They use language not only for proclamation of the *via negativa*, but for a positive expression intended to direct their disciple's mind's eye to the Inexpressible. It is not a rare occurrence to gain satori as one reads or listens to a sermon.

Zen sermons are legion; and Zen is said to have more literature than any other Buddhist sect. We have chosen sermons which serve as specimens of Japanese Zen preaching or which discuss problems of moment.

Introduction

Anecdotes

A Zen master is a man of action—action in the sense of "metaphysical" activity. He has achieved, through satori, a thorough reorientation of his whole spiritual being, and all that he utters and performs, even lifting a finger, may indicate a full accord with Absolute Nothingness. Yone Noguchi, a Japanese poet who wrote English poetry as well, eulogizes the Zennist in his poem "The Zen Priest":

> All his instincts he keeps under control,
> Flares up like a blaze in white light.

It is no wonder that masters' words and deeds have been assiduously recorded to inspire students of Zen.

Dr. Hisamatsu, an experienced lay Zennist, formerly Professor of Western Philosophy at Kyoto University, enumerates as the characteristics of Zen fine arts: asymmetry, simplicity, stark dignity, naturalness, *yugen* (subtle and graceful profundity), supramundanity, and tranquillity. These features also characterize Zen anecdotes. They will need no explanation—except perhaps their asymmetry. Asymmetry is an expression of freedom from formal balance. In the Zennist's personality it means freedom from conventional formalism; it is nonchalance of the highest order. In addition to these characteristics, the Zennist who holds a rigorous outlook on life has a high degree of generosity and leniency. Furthermore, one will often be struck by his wit and humor, qualities less commonly found in the priests of other Buddhist sects. The characteristics which distinguish the Zennist's sayings and deeds are all based on his satori, that is, Reality-intuition, or an intuitive grasp of Absolute Nothingness. In fine, what is apparent in Zen anecdotes is the masters' personal representation of Absolute Nothingness or the trainees' strenuous efforts toward its attainment.

Here again it will be of interest to compare Zennist and Christian saintliness. Zen is a godless philosophy of conduct; Christianity is a godly religion. Thence arise all the differences between the two: non-being and being, an absolutism which unites man with the All and a dualism which opposes man to God; satori and faith; zazen and prayer; koan scrutiny and spiritual exercises; naturalness and supernaturalness; no reward whatever and reward in heaven; the here-and-now viewpoint and the eschatological one. These different features necessarily are reflected in the writing and deeds of exponents of Zen and Christianity.

Interviews

With the Western reader in mind, we have exchanged general questions and answers in two interviews, each of which has a foreword; we wished to furnish him with information on genuine Zen.

In conclusion, let me cite Karl Barth. In his essay on theology (1934) he observes that a theological exegete must never treat biblical texts from his philosophical Weltanschauung. Barth fears that the exegete would otherwise distort the meaning of divine revelation. The same warning applies to the reader of Zen literature. If he desires to learn anything genuine and orthodox from it, he will have to abandon his previous view of life and religion, and give ear to what the masters say. This attitude is directly related to the respect for tradition I mentioned in the beginning of this Introduction. I have a feeling that the time is ripe for expecting as much from the Western reader of Zen literature.

Yamaguchi City, Japan   *Takashi Ikemoto*
January 1965

LET THE SPRING BREEZE ENTER:

THE QUEST OF ZEN*

In the Way of Definition

To begin, permit me to set you a koan, or Zen problem for meditation: Chased by a tiger, you jump into
an old well crawling with snakes. The vine you have
miraculously snatched and which now sustains you a
few feet from the brim of the well is being nibbled by
a mouse.

As your *roshi*,† or master, I look you straight in the
eye and demand that you tell me what you would do.
Tricky, ingenious—like most Westerners—you may very
well find a way out of the well, but none of your clever
stratagems will satisfy me. Again and again you are sent
back to the *zendo*,† or meditation hall, to ponder the
koan; it may take you as long as a year to come up with
a solution that does not disgust me. Meanwhile something is happening to you: slowly you realize that there
is no "right" answer, that all you can do while grasping
that vine for dear life (for you are living the koan) is
accept the fact that dear or not it is no longer yours.
This may make it possible for you to experience the

---

* The substance of this introduction is drawn from articles published in the *Chicago Review* and *Tri-Quarterly*.

† The terms *zendo* and *sodo* are interchangeable, as are *roshi*
and *shike*.

bliss of a satori awakening and, by so doing, understand the essence of Zen, said to be found in this four-line *gatha*:

> Transmission outside doctrine,
> No dependence on words,
> Pointing directly at the mind,
> Thus seeing oneself truly, attaining Buddhahood.

There are other, prosier ways of defining the spirit— life zest, awareness of the preciousness of each instant and every thing, a gay seriousness—but perhaps Zen is best expressed in that poetry, usually written in classical Chinese forms, which outstanding masters have traditionally composed. There is, for example, the poem by Daigu (1584–1669) from which I have drawn my title:

> Who dares approach the lion's
> Mountain cave? Cold, robust,
> A Zen-man through and through,
> I let the spring breeze enter at the gate.

It would *not* be in the spirit of Zen, which does not depend on words, to paraphrase; indeed any attempt to do so might resemble the tyro's abortive efforts with the koan above. There are some who have, through their well-meaning attempts to explain that spring breeze, well-nigh staled it for the man who would be refreshed by it. Like the famous wind of Archibald MacLeish it "Is trampled under the rain, shakes free, is again trampled." Which makes it (the spring breeze, the Spirit of Zen) something like freedom. Which is another way of saying that the *Tao*, the path, of Zen is the path of liberation.

Japanese Backgrounds

The three major sources of Japanese thought are Shinto, the indigenous religion, the Way of the Gods; Confucianism, which was of course brought over from China and was concerned with the moral ordering of society and emphasized the present; and Buddhism, the religion of eternity, which originated in India and reached Japan by way of China and Korea.

Over two thousand years old, Shinto is a national cult, the spirit of "Nippon," and it has maintained its sacred sense of nature, which according to its mythology was not made but begotten. Hence the veneration of trees, mountains, waterfalls, and the pure lines of its central shrine at Ise. Evolved from Shinto, ancient state philosophy was based on the belief in the holy oneness of man and country. There has always been in Shinto a reverence for Emperor and ancestors, and a faith in the communion of the living and the dead: there is, in other words, the sense of immortal presence.

Confucianism, on the other hand, has represented a rational, highly moral code of behavior and a system of firmly defined duties, with certain relationships—Emperor-subject, father-son, etc.—particularly upheld. And there are the practical rules of etiquette and protocol, too numerous and intricate to go into here, but of great importance to the shaping of Japanese form. Also the family system is Confucian. The rather unfortunate overspecialization in certain areas and the for-the-most-part inflexible bureaucracy (those who have seen Kurosawa's great film *Ikiru* have had a glimpse of the latter), may be the result of Confucianism, and so too the exaggerated respect shown the *sensei*, or teacher, the title held by even an instructor in ping-pong. With the master in total control of his disciple or student there has been little scope for the growth of originality as we think of it. Indeed the dismissive gesture, criticism, is in Japan the mark of a boor.

Mahayana Buddhism (the Great Wheel) has in spite of the demands of Shintoism and Confucianism dominated the Japanese mind for fifteen hundred years. All things, it claims, are predestined to become Buddhas, attain salvation. One must ignore the peculiarities of things and feel their absolute oneness. When, along with the human ego, the individuality of all is shed, then this oneness appears as emptiness. Through meditation of space can come the awakening to oneness, peace of mind, nirvana—a concept which, as Dr. D. T. Suzuki explains in his *Zen and Japanese Buddhism,* is often misunderstood:

> . . . when we talk of nirvana we imagine that there is such a thing . . . as in the case of a table or a book. Nirvana, however, is no more than a state of mind or consciousness when we actually transcend relativity—the world of birth and death.

Zen Buddhism, which since the Kamakura period (13th century), has been truly important to Japanese life and arts, from the fine to the military, *ikebana* to *kamikaze,* does not use the word God, nor (for the above reasons) does it speak of the individual soul. Various Buddhist sects, to be sure, differ in their methods of attaining salvation: in one, for instance, the mere invocation of the Buddha's name, if continuously and sincerely done, is sufficient. Other sects—Kegon, Tendai—seem more philosophical yet require, at the same

time, rather elaborate devotional devices. But whatever
the sect, because of Buddhism's "pantheism," it works
harmoniously alongside Shintoism.

In contrast to Hinayana (the Small Wheel), Mahayana Buddhism is life-loving. Even the concept of *Mu*
(nothingness) can be seen as positive, because of the
principle of unity it implies. Perhaps the main difference between the two systems is to be found in their
exemplars: the Hinayana Arhat seeks nirvana and Buddhahood fervently, whereas the Mahayana Bodhisattva
willingly postpones entering the blessed state until all
others can be saved. It is for this reason that Mahayanists offer prayers to the Savior Bodhisattva Amida.

Zen is rooted squarely in Mahayana Buddhism,
though it must not be seen as a theology. Rather it is a
system of behavior based on the desire for salvation
through revelation. What makes it virtually impene-
trable to the uninitiated is the lack of dogma as such,
and the fact that all Zen "statements" are in some manner paradoxical. Its chief practice, zazen, or formal sitting in meditation, goes back to Indian *dhyana*, and is
said to be the search, always within the seeker, for the
indivisible moon reflected not only on the sea but on
each dewdrop and, perhaps most brightly of all, on the
scummiest puddle. To discover this—the *Dharmakaya*
—in all things, is for the Zennist to discover his own
Buddha-nature.

The morality in all this is simple enough: like a tar-
nished mirror, the passion-twisted heart cannot reflect
Dharmakaya. The injunction, then? Well, clean the
mirror. By being perfect in conduct, by, as the master
Fugai (17th century) puts it in this poem, shutting the
windows of the flesh:

Only the Zen-man knows tranquillity:
The world-consuming flame can't reach this valley.
Under a breezy limb, the windows of
The flesh shut firm, I dream, wake, dream.

Zen tells that Gautama had his awakening under the
Bodhi-tree and thus became the Buddha, but few scholars have dealt adequately, if at all, with the Buddha's
early training in meditation under the tutelage of Alara
Kalama and Uddaka Ramaputta. According to Sir
Charles Eliot, in *Hinduism and Buddhism*, the first of
these great teachers instructed the Buddha in the
trances known as the formless states. The first taught
the monk in meditation to rise above all ideas of form
and multiplicity, and to pass by degrees into the sphere
where nothing at all exists, while retaining consciousness of mental processes. Buddha's second teacher
taught the attainment of a state in which neither idea
nor its absence is present, a state which can be illus-
trated, to use Sir Charles Eliot's analogy, by a bowl
whose inside has been coated with oil, a state in which
consciousness is reduced to a minimum. As is well
known, the Buddha was to reject those teachings which
made hypnotic trances their chief aim.

Though perhaps too much has been made of it by
the followers of Dr. Suzuki, there is no questioning
Zen's similarity to mysticism. There is, for example, the
Zen saying that the eye of divinity can be seen in a lotus blossom. In the same vein, that incredible German
Meister Eckhart said, "The eye with which I see God
is the eye with which God sees me." Instead of seeking
God, Zen's adherents seek, and through zazen and its
aim, satori, sometimes find, nirvana. And they find the

Way not by learning, but while in meditation, in the *tanden*, the body's exact center.

Philosophy and Zen

Those who should know, maintain that Western philosophy received its greatest impetus at about the time of the Enlightenment in the eighteenth century, when having lost faith in religion's ready answers to the big questions, man tried on his own to fathom the only world he was ever likely to know. In a completely religious culture there would be little need for philosophy, because all answers would be supplied by dogma.

The most complete philosophers are those able to cope most thoroughly with the deepest problems: Kant, for example, with his Categorical Imperatives to guide conduct and his *Kosmos* to prefigure an essentially atomistic universe. Some thinkers have of course worked in a more fragmentary way—there are philosophical lyrics as well as epics—but, fragmentary or all-embracing, Western philosophy does not greatly interest the Zennist.

This lack of interest, it should be made clear at once, is not to be attributed to lack of curiosity, nor should it be seen as the result of religious thralldom. So far as Zen is concerned, it is just that most of the questions asked by Western thinkers are either frivolous or, worse, impertinent. If posed at all by a master, they are pondered in a very different manner, as in the case of the koan, for the mind, it is thought, severely limited and conditioned powerfully by egoistic needs, is simply not to be relied on in crucial issues. Intuition, mysterious as it may be, has always been considered by the Zennist a truer way of discovery, less a toying with the world.

Revelation of the kind sought by the Zennist is not to be confused with the Christian sort: for one thing, one need not be sporting a halo to experience it. Yet it often takes a superhuman effort:

Kando (1825–1904)

It's as if our heads were on fire, the way
We apply ourselves to perfection of That.
The future but a twinkle, beat yourself,
Persist: the greatest effort's not enough.

But when there is an awakening:

Tsugen (1322–1391)

Not a mote in the light above,
Soul itself cannot offer such a view.
Though dawn's not come, the cock is calling:
The phoenix, flower in beak, welcomes spring.

Always Zen is to be found, if at all, in immediate experience, the firefly rather than the star.

In Zen aesthetics there is a clear parallel to phenomenology. When, following Kierkegaard, Existentialists speak of the need to leap from one state of awareness —commitment—to another, higher, state they are saying what the Zen masters have always said. The *sumie* painter, perhaps without training in Zen but heir to its treasures, raises brush over blankness and at just the right moment takes such a leap into a free and floating world.

"The form of the object must first fuse with the spirit," wrote the great fifth-century Chinese painter Wang Wei* "after which the mind transforms it in

* Mai-Mai Sze, *The Tao of Painting*, Pantheon Books, 1956.

various ways. The spirit, to be sure, has no form; yet that which moves and transforms the form of an object is the spirit."

That life is most vivid to one on the brink of death is a truism. The subjects of sumie painting—flower, rock, mountain, perhaps a human figure—are severely defined against the white background, thus taking on strong existential meaning. To most Japanese, certainly to those interested in Zen, the background clearly represents death, the reality of man facing annihilation, fully aware of his *mujo*, or impermanence.

In the literature conditioned by Zen there is also a sense of this nothingness against which the mortal drama unfolds, as in Yasunari Kawabata's fine modern novel *Yukiguni*. Indeed the translator of the English version (*Snow Country*, Charles E. Tuttle Co.), Edward G. Seidensticker, relates the technique of the book to the haiku, the seventeen-syllable poems that have long been associated with Zen: "The *haiku* manner," he writes in a perceptive introduction to the book, "is notable for its terseness and austerity, so that [the novelist's work] must rather be like a series of brief flashes in a void." Then there are the early Noh plays, perfect in their expression of Zen, and the dramas of Chikamatsu Monzaemon, the eighteenth-century Japanese Shakespeare, so-called, full, among other things, of the anguish of lovers about to commit suicide.

Japanese suicide, or hara-kiri, has much Zen in it, it would seem, for when a man finds himself faced, through an awakening sought or unsought, with the absurdity of his lot, he may decide coldly to make as honorable an end as possible by taking the existential leap—into the grave. One thinks of the forty-seven Ronin, those fearless samurai who committed hara-kiri at the command of the Tokugawa Shogun nearly three hundred years ago; of the astonishing love suicides of the 1930s; and most remarkable, of those ten members of the ultranationalist Japan Productive Party, who on August 22, 1945, a week after the end of World War II, sat in a circle in downtown Tokyo and, while chanting apologies to the Emperor for losing the war, pulled pins from hand grenades and blew themselves to bits (less than a week later, three of their widows went to the same spot and shot themselves to death). Not as dramatic, perhaps, but of far greater importance to Zen, which, after all, has never condoned suicide, is the stoic death:

> *Baiho* (1633–1707)
>
> Never giving thought to fame,
> One troublesome span of life behind,
> Cross-legged in the coffin,
> I'm about to slough the flesh.

"If instead of the paradisiacal bliss promised by your faith," I was once asked by a Japanese student trained in Zen, "you were threatened with a chain of rebirths, each with its portion of misery, until by some superhuman act you were able to snap that chain, would you not make every effort to order your life so as to be able to live it fully, now, while you have it?" In so bleak a scheme of things, the implication must be drawn: there is small reason for the rapturous faith many profess. Yet there is a way out: unswerving acceptance of the reality of self. Existence, of which for ages a single image has been held up to the Zennist, must be adjusted to: it cannot be altered. His training in the zendo, all rituals of his life, are meant to help him make that adjustment.

The Uses (and Abuses) of Zen

In the course of one of the interviews included in this book, with Taigan Takayama, I ask whether Zen can be used by artists, as it might have been by the great master painter Sesshu, to achieve the proper state of mind for serious artistic production. The master's answer: "Zen is not something to be used. Zen art is nothing more than an expression of a Zen state of mind." But this is the subject that most interests me, and I have the temerity to pursue it: "Well, then, how would you describe that state of mind, as it relates, that is, to the artist and his work? And though here I may be asking too much, would you say that artists—painters, writers, composers—might gain by periods of discipline? And if so, what have they to gain, that drink or, to be more consistent, prayer and the seeking of vision might not be able to afford with less difficulty?" To this Taigan Takayama answers: "Let's put it this way: it is a state of mind in which one is identified with an object without any sense of restraint." Which of course echoes the words of Wang Wei, written some fifteen hundred years ago, already quoted.

"Can one pluck the flower which is Zen, and transplant it, rootless, to an alien shore?" asks Dom Aelred Graham in his *Zen Catholicism*.* "It seems improbable," he goes on to answer the question. "The attempt to do so may account for some of the oddities, not to say frivolities, attending the current interest in Zen."

What in fact are these oddities, frivolities, these new Japanesqueries? The aesthetics of the Beats and the action painters of a certain camp, the rehashes of Dr.

* Harcourt, Brace & World, 1964.

Suzuki that one can pick up at the corner drug store? But, if so, what must one conclude about Ezra Pound and Imagism, about W. B. Yeats's "ancient blade, still as it was, / Still razor-keen, still like a looking-glass / Unspotted by the centuries"? Is it their fame that saves Pound and Yeats from chastisement, or the fact that they were early on the scene? Surely it was the Zen in Japanese art that attracted them.

Whatever it is the author of *Zen Catholicism* has in mind, there is no question of Zen's current modishness, resembling existentialism's in the late '40s (*item:* in December 1962 A *Tenth of an Inch Makes a Difference*, three plays based on Zen folklore and anecdotes, was given at the East End Theatre in New York). Thus, presumably, the reaction. Indeed there is a new game, Kick-Zen, at which those in the forefront of the reaction, a few of whom reign as stars of the literary quarterlies, are becoming quite expert. But it is a game, a friend recently observed, that a true Zennist would be very much inclined to enjoy.

If the Beat poets find stimulation in Zen, fine; if the action painters interested in Zen calligraphy are led to a few minor discoveries, we all stand to gain; if the rehashers of Dr. Suzuki provide us, if only fortuitously and because they bring Western sensibilities to the subject, with a couple of novel ideas, well, why complain? The one free world is the world of the mind, which is something we had better not forget.

Yet a certain amount of obfuscation has resulted, and there is a real need to cross the faddish peripheries and get as close to the heart of Zen as possible, the writings of the masters. It is that which along with others Takashi Ikemoto and I are attempting to do. And in publishing what follows it is our hope that the reader will be helped in his quest for freedom, which is the historical quest of Zen.

Lucien Stryk

POEMS

ZEN POEMS: TRANSLATIONS FROM THE JAPANESE MASTERS

DOGEN (1200–1253, Soto)

The Western Patriarch's doctrine is transplanted!
I fish by moonlight, till on cloudy days.
Clean, clean! Not a worldy mote falls with the snow
As, cross-legged in this mountain hut, I sit the evening
   through.

DOGEN, *waka*

Coming, going, the waterfowl
Leaves not a trace,
Nor does it need a guide.

A waka on "The mind must operate without abiding anywhere"
(from the *Diamond Sutra*).

SHOICHI (1202–1280, Rinzai)

The all-meaning circle:
No in, no out;
No light, no shade.
Here all saints are born.

Circle. Symbol of the Buddha-nature, the Way, etc. This poem
accompanies a drawing by the poet. Sometimes a master will make
a circle with his hand or staff, the symbolism being clear to all.

3

RYUZAN (1274–1358, Rinzai)

Clear in the blue, the moon!
Icy water to the horizon,
Defining high, low. Startled,
The dragon uncoils about the billows.

GASAN (1275–1365, Soto)

Invaluable is the Soto Way—
Why be discipline's slave?
Snapping the golden chain,
Step boldly toward the sunset!

MUSO (1275–1351, Rinzai)

Many times the mountains have turned from green to
　　　yellow—
So much for the capricious earth!
Dust in your eyes, the triple world is narrow;
Nothing on the mind, your chair is wide enough.

MUSO, *satori poem*

Vainly I dug for a perfect sky,
Piling a barrier all around.
Then one black night, lifting a heavy
Tile, I crushed the skeletal void!

Poems

DAITO (1282–1337, Rinzai), *satori poem*

At last I've broken Unmon's barrier!
There's exit everywhere—east, west; north, south.
In at morning, out at evening; neither host nor guest.
My every step stirs up a little breeze.

   Unmon's barrier is to be found in the eighth koan of *Heki-ganroku*, which Daito succeeded in solving. Unmon (–966) was a great Chinese master. "Unmon's barrier" also suggests the "cloud barrier," making the poem all the more graphic.

DAITO, *death poem*

To slice through Buddhas, Patriarchs
I grip my polished sword.
One glance at my mastery,
The void bites its tusks!

GETSUDO (1285–1361, Rinzai), *satori poem*

I moved across the Dharma-nature,
The earth was buoyant, marvelous.
That very night, whipping its iron horse,
The void galloped into Cloud Street.

DAICHI (1290–1366, Soto)

Thoughts arise endlessly,
There's a span to every life.
One hundred years, thirty-six thousand days:
The spring through, the butterfly dreams.

JAKUSHITSU (1290–1367, Rinzai)

Refreshing, the wind against the waterfall
As the moon hangs, a lantern, on the peak
And the bamboo window glows. In old age mountains
Are more beautiful than ever. My resolve:
That these bones be purified by rocks.

CHIKUSEN (1292–1348, Soto)

He's part of all, yet all's transcended;
Solely for convenience he's known as master.
Who dares say he's found him?
In this rackety town I train disciples.

BETSUGEN (1294–1369, Rinzai)

All night long I think of life's labyrinth—
Impossible to visit the tenants of Hades.
The authoritarian attempt to palm a horse off as deer
Was laughable. As was the thrust at
The charmed life of the dragon. Contemptible!
It's in the dark that eyes probe earth and heaven,
In dream that the tormented seek present, past.
Enough! The mountain moon fills the window.
The lonely fall through, the garden rang with cricket
    song.

The authoritarian attempt . . . refers to the Chinese classic
Shiki, in which Choko presents a horse to the Emperor, claiming
it is a deer. The Emperor's courtiers, obsequious to Choko, do
not dispute his claim.

As was the thrust at . . . refers to Soshi (Chuantzu): Shu
spent three years acquiring the skill to kill dragons, but of course
this did him no good.

Poems

JUO (1296–1380, Rinzai)

Beyond the snatch of time, my daily life.
I scorn the State, unhitch the universe.
Denying cause and effect, like the noon sky,
My up-down career: Buddhas nor Patriarchs
    can convey it.

FUMON (1302–1369, Rinzai), *death poem*

Magnificent! Magnificent!
No-one knows the final word.
The ocean bed's aflame,
Out of the void leap wooden lambs.

SHUTAKU (1308–1388, Rinzai)

For all these years, my certain Zen:
Neither I nor the world exist.
The sutras neat within the box,
My cane hooked upon the wall,
I lie at peace in moonlight
Or, hearing water plashing on the rock,
Sit up: none can purchase pleasure such as this:
Spangled across the step-moss, a million coins!

~~~~~

Mind set free in the Dharma-realm,
I sit at the moon-filled window
Watching the mountains with my ears,
Hearing the stream with open eyes.
Each molecule preaches perfect law,
Each moment chants true sutra:
The most fleeting thought is timeless,
A single hair's enough to stir the sea.

7

RYUSHU (1308–1388, Rinzai)

Why bother with the world?
Let others go gray, bustling east, west.
In this mountain temple, lying half-in,
Half-out, I'm removed from joy and sorrow.

SHUNOKU (1311–1388, Rinzai)

After the spring song, "Vast emptiness, no holiness,"
Comes the song of snow-wind along the Yangtze River.
Late at night I too play the noteless flute of Shorin,
Piercing the mountains with its sound, the river.

Vast emptiness, no holiness. Bodhidharma's reply to the question put by Butei, Emperor of Ryo, "What is the primary principle of Buddhism?" (Cf. the first koan of *Hekiganroku.*)
Shorin. Name of the temple where Bodhidharma, on finding that Butei was not a true Zennist, sat in Zen for nine years. To reach the temple, he had to cross the Yangtze River.

TESSHU (14th century, Rinzai)

How heal the phantom body of its phantom ill,
Which started in the womb?
Unless you pluck a medicine from the Bodhi-tree,
The sense of karma will destroy you.

TSUGEN (1322–1391, Soto)

Not a mote in the light above,
Soul itself cannot offer such a view.
Though dawn's not come, the cock is calling:
The phoenix, flower in beak, welcomes spring.

GUCHU (1323–1409, Rinzai)

Men without rank, excrement spatulas,
Come together, perfuming earth and heaven.
How well they get along in temple calm
As, minds empty, they reach for light.

Excrement spatulas. To a monk's question, "What is the
Buddha?", Unmon replied, "An excrement spatula." (Cf. the
twenty-first koan of *Mumonkan*.)

MUNON (1323–1390, Rinzai)

Life: a cloud crossing the peak.
Death: the moon sailing.
Oh just once admit the truth
Of noumenon, phenomenon,
And you're a donkey-tying pole!

A donkey-tying pole. Often used in Zen writing, meaning a
trifle.

GIDO (1325–1388, Rinzai): *Inscription over His Door*

He who holds that nothingness
Is formless, flowers are visions,
Let him enter boldly!

KUKOKU (1328–1407, Rinzai), *death poem*

Riding this wooden upside-down horse,
I'm about to gallop through the void.
Would you seek to trace me?
Ha! Try catching the tempest in a net.

ZEKKAI (1336–1405, Rinzai), *death poem*

The void has collapsed upon the earth,
Stars, burning, shoot across Iron Mountain.
Turning a somersault, I brush past.

Iron Mountain. Cakravala, a great mountain in ancient Indian cosmology.

REIZAN (–1411, Rinzai)

The myriad differences resolved by sitting, all doors
    opened.
In this still place I follow my nature, be what it may.
From the one hundred flowers I wander freely,
The soaring cliff—my hall of meditation
(With the moon emerged, my mind is motionless).
Sitting on this frosty seat, no further dream of fame.
The forest, the mountain follow their ancient ways,
And through the long spring day, not even the shadow
    of a bird.

MYOYU (1333–1393, Soto), *satori poem*

Defying the power of speech, the Law Commission on
    Mount Vulture!
Kasyapa's smile told the beyond-telling.
What's there to reveal in that perfect all-suchness?
Look up! the moon-mind glows unsmirched.

EICHU (1340–1416, Soto), *satori poem*

My eyes eavesdrop on their lashes!
I'm finished with the ordinary!
What use has halter, bridle
To one who's shaken off contrivance?

Poems

Hakugai (1343–1414, Rinzai), *satori poem*

Last year in a lovely temple in Hirosawa,
This year among the rocks of Nikko,
All's the same to me:
Clapping hands, the peaks roar at the blue!

Nanei (1363–1438, Rinzai)

Splitting the void in half,
Making smithereens of earth,
I watch inching toward
The river, the cloud-drawn moon.

Kodo (1370–1433, Rinzai)

Serving the Shogun in the capital,
Stained by worldly dust, I found no peace.
Now, straw hat pulled down, I follow the river:
How fresh the sight of gulls across the sand!

Bokuo (1384–1455, Rinzai), *death poem*

For seventy-two years
I've kept the ox well under.
Today, the plum in bloom again,
I let him wander in the snow.

Ox. An animal closely connected with Zen. In this poem it
serves as an object of discipline.

Ikkyu (1394–1481, Rinzai)

After ten years in the red-light district,
How solitary a spell in the mountains.
I can see clouds a thousand miles away,
Hear ancient music in the pines.

11

Void in Form

When, just as they are,
White dewdrops gather
On scarlet maple leaves,
Regard the scarlet beads!

A waka on "Void in Form" (from *The Heart Sutra*).

Form in Void

The tree is stripped,
All color, fragrance gone,
Yet already on the bough,
Uncaring spring!

A waka on "Form in Void" (from *The Heart Sutra*).

KOKAI (1403–1469, Rinzai), *satori poem*

Taking hold, one's astray in nothingness;
Letting go, the Origin's regained.
Since the music stopped, no shadow's touched
My door: again the village moon's above the river.

NENSHO (1409–1482, Soto)

Only genuine awakening results in *that*.
Only fools seek sainthood for reward.
Lifting a hand, the stone lantern announces daybreak.
Smiling, the void nods its enormous head.

GENKO (–1505, Soto)

Unaware of illusion or enlightenment,
From this stone I watch the mountains, hear the
    stream.
A three-day rain has cleansed the earth,
A roar of thunder split the sky.
Ever serene are linked phenomena,
And though the mind's alert, it's but an ash heap.
Chilly, bleak as the dusk I move through,
I return, a basket brimmed with peaches on my arm.

SAISHO (–1506, Rinzai): *On Joshu's Nothingness*

Earth, mountains, rivers—hidden in this nothingness.
In this nothingness—earth, mountains, rivers revealed.
Spring flowers, winter snows:
There's no being nor non-being, nor denial itself.

YUISHUN (–1544, Soto), *satori poem*

Why, it's but the motion of eyes and brows!
And here I've been seeking it far and wide.
Awakened at last, I find the moon
Above the pines, the river surging high.

TAKUAN (1573–1645, Rinzai), *waka*

Though night after night
The moon is stream-reflected,
Try to find where it has touched,
Point even to a shadow.

A waka on "The willow is green, the rose is red."

GUDO (1579–1659, Rinzai)

It's not nature that upholds utility.
Look! even the rootless tree is swelled
With bloom, not red nor white, but lovely all the same.
How many can boast so fine a springtide?

UNGO (1580–1659, Rinzai)

Whirled by the three passions, one's eyes go blind;
Closed to the world of things, they see again.
In this way I live: straw-hatted, staff in hand,
I move illimitably, through earth, through heaven.

DAIGU (1584–1669, Rinzai)

Here none think of wealth or fame,
All talk of right and wrong is quelled:
In autumn I rake the leaf-banked stream,
In spring attend the nightingale.

Who dares approach the lion's
Mountain cave? Cold, robust,
A Zen-man through and through,
I let the spring breeze enter at the gate.

MANAN (1591–1654, Soto)

Unfettered at last, a traveling monk,
I pass the old Zen barrier.
Mine is a traceless stream-and-cloud life.
Of those mountains, which shall be my home?

Poems

FUGAI (17th century, Soto)

Only the Zen-man knows tranquillity:
The world-consuming flame can't reach this valley.
Under a breezy limb, the windows of
The flesh shut firm, I dream, wake, dream.

BUNAN (1602–1676, Rinzai), *waka*

The moon's the same old moon,
The flowers exactly as they were,
Yet I've become the thingness
Of all the things I see!

BUNAN, *waka*

When you're both alive and dead,
Thoroughly dead to yourself,
How superb
The smallest pleasure!

KARASUMARU-MITSUHIRO (1579–1638, Rinzai)

Beware of gnawing the ideogram of nothingness:
Your teeth will crack. Swallow it whole, and you've
    a treasure
Beyond the hope of Buddha and the Mind. The east
    breeze
Fondles the horse's ears: how sweet the smell of plum.

TOSUI (–1683, Soto)

Content with chipped bowl and tattered robe,
My life moves on serenely.
The single task: allaying hunger, thirst,
Indifferent to the murmurous world.

GESSHU (1618–1696, Soto), *satori poem*

The seven seas sucked up together,
The dragon god's exposed.
Backwards flows the stream of Soto Zen:
Enlightened at last, I breathe!

BAIHO (1633–1707, Soto): *On Entering His Coffin*

Never giving thought to fame,
One troublesome span of life behind,
Cross-legged in the coffin,
I'm about to slough the flesh.

MANZAN (1635–1714, Rinzai)

One minute of sitting, one inch of Buddha.
Like lightning all thoughts come and pass.
Just once look into your mind-depths:
Nothing else has ever been.

TOKUO (1649–1709, Rinzai)

The town's aflame with summer heat,
But Mount Koma is steeped in snow.
Such is a Zen-man's daily life—
The lotus survives all earthly fire.

HAKUIN (1685–1768, Rinzai)

Past, present, future: unattainable,
Yet clear as the moteless sky.
Late at night the stool's cold as iron,
But the moonlit window smells of plum.

~~~~~

Priceless is one's incantation,
Turning a red-hot iron ball to butter oil.
Heaven? Purgatory? Hell?
Snowflakes fallen on the hearth fire.

~~~~~

How lacking in permanence the minds of the sentient—
They are the consummate nirvana of all Buddhas.
A wooden hen, egg in mouth, straddles the coffin.
An earthenware horse breaks like wind for satori-land.

~~~~~

You no sooner attain the great void
Than body and mind are lost together.
Heaven and Hell—a straw.
The Buddha-realm, Pandemonium—shambles.
Listen: a nightingale strains her voice, serenading the
     snow.
Look: a tortoise wearing a sword climbs the lampstand.
Should you desire the great tranquillity,
Prepare to sweat white beads.

SENGAI (1750–1837, Rinzai): *On Basho's "Frog"*

Under the cloudy cliff, near the temple door,
Between dusky spring plants on the pond,
A frog jumps in the water, plop!
Startled, the poet drops his brush.

   Basho's haiku on the frog is one of the most famous ever written. Here is Harold G. Henderson's translation (*An Introduction
to Haiku*, Doubleday Anchor):
                    Old pond—
                        and a frog-jump-in
                     water-sound.

RYOKAN (1757–1831, Rinzai)

Without a jot of ambition left
I let my nature flow where it will.
There are ten days of rice in my bag
And, by the hearth, a bundle of firewood.
Who prattles of illusion or nirvana?
Forgetting the equal dusts of name and fortune,
Listening to the night rain on the roof of my hut,
I sit at ease, both legs stretched out.

KANEMITSU-KOGUN (18th century)

My hands released at last, the cliff soars
Ten thousand meters, the plowshare sparks,
All's consumed with my body. Born again,
The lanes run straight, the rice well in the ear.

KOSEN (1808–1893, Rinzai), *satori poem*

A blind horse trotting up an icy ledge—
Such is the poet. Once disburdened
Of those frog-in-the-well illusions,
The sutra-store's a lamp against the sun.

TANZAN (1819–1892, Soto)

Madness, the way they gallop off to foreign shores!
Turning to the One Mind, I find my Buddhahood,
Above self and others, beyond coming and going.
This will remain when all else is gone.

KANDO (1825–1904, Rinzai)

It's as if our heads were on fire, the way
We apply ourselves to perfection of That.
The future but a twinkle, beat yourself,
Persist: the greatest effort's not enough.

NANTEMBO (1839–1925, Rinzai): *On New Year's Day*

Fresh in their new wraps, earth and heaven,
And today I greet my eighty-first spring.
Ambition burning still, I grip my nandin staff.
Cutting through all, I spin the Wheel of Law.

SODO (1841–1920, Soto)

The question clear, the answer deep,
Each particle, each instant a reality,
A bird call shrills through mountain dawn:
Look where the old master sits, a rock, in Zen.

MOKUSEN (1847–1920, Soto): *On Climbing
the Mountain Where Buddha Trained*

However difficult the cliff,
It's only after climbing one's aware.
Leisurely I followed Tathagata's footsteps.
Roaring below, a tiger chilled the day.

SOEN (1859–1919, Rinzai)

Calm, activity—each has its use. At times
This worldly dust piles mountain-high.
Now the neighbor's asleep, I chant a sutra.
The incense burnt away, I sing before the moon.

Master Joshu and the dog—
Truly exorbitant, their foolishness.
Being and non-being at last
Annihilated, speak the final word!

*On Visiting Shorin Temple, Where Bodhidharma
Once Lived*

The steep slope hangs above
The temple calm. An autumn voyager,
I go by ways neither old nor new,
Finding east, west my mind the same.

TESSHU (1879–1939, Rinzai): *On Visiting Sokei,
Where the Sixth Patriarch (632–712) Lived*

The holy earth is overspread with leaves,
Wind crosses a thousand miles of autumn fields.
The moon that brushes Mount Sokei silvers,
This very instant, far Japan.

Shinkichi Takahashi (1901–   , Rinzai): *The Peach*

A little girl under a peach tree,
Whose blossoms fall into the entrails
Of the earth.

There you stand, but a mountain may be there
Instead; it is not unlikely that the earth
May be yourself.

You step against a plate of iron and half
Your face is turned to iron. I will smash
Flesh and bone

And suck the cracked peach. She went up the mountain
To hide her breasts in the snowy ravine.
Women's legs

Are more or less alike. The leaves of the peach tree
Stretch across the sea to the end of
The continent.

The sea was at the little girl's beck and call.
I will cross the sea like a hairy
Caterpillar

And catch the odor of your body.

Quails

It is the grass that moves, not the quails.
Weary of embraces, she thought of
Committing her body to the flame.

When I shut my eyes, I hear far and wide
The air of the Ice Age stirring.
When I open them, a rocket passes over a meteor.

A quail's egg is complete in itself,
Leaving not room enough for a dagger's point.
All the phenomena in the universe: myself.

Quails are supported by the universe
(I wonder if that means subsisting by God).
A quail has seized God by the neck

With its black bill, because there is no
God greater than a quail.
(Peter, Christ, Judas: a quail.)

A quail's egg: idle philosophy in solution.
(There is no wife better than a quail.)
I dropped a quail's egg into a cup for buckwheat
      noodles,

And made havoc of the Democratic Constitution.
Split chopsticks stuck in the back, a quail husband
Will deliver dishes on a bicycle, anywhere.

The light yellow legs go up the hill of Golgotha.
Those quails who stood on the rock, became the rock!
The nightfall is quiet, but inside the congealed exuviae

Numberless insects zigzag, on parade.

Horse

Young girls bloom like flowers.
Unharnessed, a horse trots
Round its driver who
Grasps it by a rope.

Far off a horse is going round and round
In a square plot.

Not miserable, not cheerful either,
The bay horse is prancing,
Shaking its head, throwing up its legs
By turn: it is not running.

But there are no spectators
In what looks like an amphitheater.

White cherry petals fall like snowflakes
In the wind. All at once,
Houses, people vanish, into silence.
Nothing moves. Streetcars, buses, are held back
Silently. Quiet, everything.
All visible things become this nothingness.

The horse's bones—beautiful in their gray sheen.

A horse is going round and round,
Dancing now, with *joie de vivre*,
Under the cliff of death.

Sun

Stretched in the genial sun
The mountain snake
Tickled its length along the rock.

The wind rustled the sunshine,
But the snake,
Fully uncoiled, was calm.

Fifty thousand years ago!
Later the same sun
Blazed across the pyramids,

Now it warms my chest.
But below, through
Shattered rock, the snake

Thrusts up its snout, fangs
Flicking at my thoughts
Strewn about the rocks like violets.

It's you, faces cut like triangles,
Have kept the snake alive!
The pavement's greened with leaves.

Bream

What's land? What's water?
In the window of the florist
Swims the big-eyed bream,
Between dahlias, chrysanthemums.

So you're alone? Well, forget
Others, keep talking to yourself.
Past the hydrangea leaves
Sways the scaly bream-mass.

History? Look between
The dry leaves of the sardine
Paper. Oops! the anemone's
Finally snagged a scale,

And flowering on a tulip stem,
The bream's tail and fin!
Why fear? What do you know
Of what happens after death?

Just remember to pierce
The cactus through your Christmas hat.
Brushed by trumpet lilies, roses,
The bream opens/shuts his mouth.

The Position of the Sparrow

The sparrow has cut the day in half:
Afternoons—yesterday's, the day after tommorow's—
Layer the white wall.
Those of last year, and next year's too,
Are dyed into the wall—see them?—
And should the wall come down,
Why, those afternoons will remain,
Glimmering, just as they are, through time.

(That was a colorless realm where,
Nevertheless, most any color could well up.)

Just as the swan becomes a crow,
So everything improves—everything:
No evil *can* persist, and as to things,
Why, nothing is unchangeable.
The squirrel, for instance, is on the tray,
Buffalos lumber through African brush,
The snail wends along the wall,
Leaving a silver trail.
The sparrow's bill grips a pomegranate seed:
Just anything can resemble a lens, or a squirrel.

Because the whole is part, there's not a whole,
Anywhere, that is not part.
And all those happenings a billion years ago,
Are happening now, all around us: time.
Indeed this morning the sparrow hopped about
In that nebulous whirlpool
A million light years hence.

And since the morning is void,
Anything can be. Since mornings
A billion years from now are nothingness,
We can behold them.
The sparrow stirs,
The universe moves slightly.

Deck

If time is but a stream flowing from past to future,
Why, it's nothing more than sardine guts!
If all is carried away by it,
Then everything is seaweed along a desolate strand!
Has this stream no end at all?
Then there ought to be an unmapped sea around it.

The tide moves at its own sweet will,
Yet whether it moves or not—who cares?
Still, an absolutely immobile ship is by the quay:
Should its anchor drop to the depths of time,
We'll have had it, the harbor will dry up.

A sailor goes ashore, walking along
With existence in the palm of his hand.
With nothing under him,
His tapering toes extend,
Then—like a meteor—disappear.

The sailor is free to go anywhere,
No deck is bigger than his hand.

The Cloud and the Butterfly

The idea that's just popped into my head
Is that butterfly settled
On the field's warped bamboo fence.

At times it just gathers wings and rests,
Then flits wildly about the field:
The fence has nothing to do with the butterfly,
I have nothing to do with my idea.

Go dig in the field, you won't find me:
I'm neither field nor fence.

There's a white cloud above,
But I'm not that either.
The cloud? It seeks the butterfly
Which, wings folded, lies on the cold ground.

Black Smoke

I have thrown my "me" away:
The river willows bud pale blue.

Where did I toss that "me"?
I sought it in wind and water.

Resigned, I looked up:
A cat at the controls of a helicopter!

Landing and sidling up to me,
Where I lay flat on my back, he asked:

"Have you emerged from the earth—you?"

"Who—me?"

"Well then, what's that grass sprouting
All over your behind?"

Out shot my hand and grabbed
The cat's tail, which I was still holding
When the helicopter went up again.

At last I had found my "me,"
I thought, but not for long.

Night fell silently, but high above
Two glittering eyeballs wouldn't disappear.

They were burning on me,
As if the "me" I'd abandoned,
Overpowered by loneliness,
Was frantically craving me.

Oh, I understood that those eyeballs
Might have been the cat's—
How she must have suffered without her tail!

I lit a cigarette, black smoke rose,
Then I quickly buried it.

Then came a most marvelous idea:
Even if I didn't find my "me,"
I'd still have my tail!

Mascot

Somebody is breathing inside me—
Birds, the very earth.

The ocean's in my chest. Walking,
I always throw myself down.

Newssheets, a puppy were dancing in the wind—
Trucks rushed by,

Empty trucks stout enough to carry the earth
On their puncture-proof tires.

The instant I raised my hand to wave,
I was nowhere.

The puppy was sprawled out on its belly,
Run over—again, again.

You're a badger, I'll bet, posing as a mascot
With that moonlit tie

And, sticking from your pocket, night's flower.

Stitches

My wife is always knitting, knitting:
Not that I watch her,
Not that I know what she thinks.

(Awake till dawn
I drowned in your eyes—
I must be dead:
Perhaps it's the mind that stirs.)

With that bamboo needle
She knits all space, piece by piece,
Hastily hauling time in.

Brass-cold, exhausted,
She drops into bed and,
Breathing calmly, falls asleep.

Her dream must be deepening,
Her knitting coming loose.

Comet

A word swims through the air—
Fish; vomited dust speck;
Jet through the sound barrier,
Full of Thames fog.
How far is it flying?

A man wrings out a casting net
In the upper reaches of the Milky Way:
Rain pours through his brains,
Cliffs reveal themselves.

The sun, ah the sun, is dissolved
In blue, and now seer and seen
Are one: wet, smoky.

There were no rocks around,
The word plunged down the precipice—
Now blanched, dead,
Mere time carcass, it sways
Like seaweed on the beach.

Its eyes devoured by crows,
The waves splash over it.

Then as from inside a violoncello
Someone said to himself:
"The sun is hidden
In a single sand grain."

An airfield too luxuriant with word endings,
Contact of white and black clouds
Followed by thunder—
The birth of new figures.

The moment it is announced
It rises with the globe
Into the stratosphere,
Up to the shores of constellations,
The word.

Snail

The snail crawls over blackness.

Just now, in the garden,
A solid lump of snow
Slipped from the zinc roof
To behead the nandin.

Make it snappy!

In full view a stalk has been
Torn off:
Let the wind rage over the earth,
He is unaware.

His head flies to the end
Of the world,
His body is tossed
Into the ash can.

Could it be that he's the falling snow?

Fish

I hold a newspaper, reading.
Suddenly my hands become cow ears,
Then turn into Pusan, the South Korean port.

Lying on a mat
Spread on the bankside stones,
I fell asleep.
But a willow leaf, breeze-stirred,
Brushed my ear.
I remained just as I was,
Near the murmurous water.

When young there was a girl
Who became a fish for me.
Whenever I wanted fish
Broiled in salt, I'd summon her.
She'd get down on her stomach
To be sun-cooked on the stones.
And she was always ready!

Alas, she no longer comes to me.
An old benighted drake,
I hobble homeward.
But look, my drake feet become horse hoofs!
Now they drop off
And, stretching marvelously,
Become the tracks of the Tokaido Railway Line.

PRAYERS AND SERMONS

PRAYERS

I. DAICHI (1290–1366, Soto)

Daichi gained satori after seven years of training under Keizan when he chanced to see a monk passing along the temple corridor. At the age of twenty-five he sailed to China, remaining ten years and being warmly received wherever he preached. After returning to Japan he succeeded Meiho, on Keizan's recommendation. Most of his last years were spent at a beautiful mountain retreat, which inspired him to write poetry. Indeed he is one of the greatest priest-poets in the history of Japanese Zen, "Master Daichi's Poetry" being very popular with the readers of Zen verse.

My one desire is to dedicate this body born of my parents to the vow-ocean of Buddha, Law and Order. May I in all bodily actions be fully in accord with the holy rules, cherishing Buddha's Law throughout the rounds of birth and death until my reincarnation as a Buddha. May I never grow tired of saving all that is sentient wherever I happen to be. May I ever be masterful, whether in the forest of spears, the mountain of swords, the boiling caldron, or the heap of burning coals, always bearing the Treasure of the Correct-Law Eye. May Buddha, Law and Order testify to my faith! May Buddhas and patriarchs safeguard me!

II. Bassui (1327–1387, Rinzai)

Bassui entered the priesthood at twenty-nine, a comparatively late age, though he had had some measure of spiritual illumination. He experienced an important awakening on hearing the rush of a mountain stream. Though his insight was much admired by several masters, he was not satisfied with himself and chose to undergo more discipline with another master, Koho. One day Koho asked him, "Why did Joshu utter the word 'Mu'?" Bassui was about to answer when the master cried out, "Don't use your mind!" On hearing these words, Bassui attained perfect satori, and later he was to become Koho's successor. The following is an example of his very free manner of treating Zen *mondo* (question and answer):

> Monk: All is reduced to One. What is this One reduced to?
> Bassui: One inch long, one hundred meters short.
> Monk: I can't understand.
> Bassui: Go and take some tea.

He taught and enlightened people in all walks of life by saying this prayer, composed when he was quite young.

May I, with clear *Marga* (truth) -eye, inherit the wisdom of Buddhas and patriarchs and, training superior beings, pitying those in error, conduct men and devas along the road to enlightenment. If any be so unlucky as to fall into the three hells—fire, blood, swords—I will suffer for him. Should the torment last a hundred million *kalpas* (aeons), I will not retreat.

SERMONS

I. DOGEN (1200–1253, Soto)

Dogen, founder of the Japanese Soto sect, one of
the most influential Buddhist sects in the country,
was a child prodigy who not only read the Chinese
classics but composed poems in Chinese. His father, a
courtier of high rank, died when Dogen was three
years old; his mother died when he was eight. In spite
of his relatives' opposition, he decided to renounce
the world, and at fourteen he became a bonze and a
disciple of Eizai, who unfortunately died not long after. He trained with Myozen, Eizai's disciple, and
went to China in his twenty-fourth year. There he visited a number of prominent masters, but none satisfied him. He was about to leave China in great disap-
pointment when he heard of a Soto master, Nyojo.
Dogen found him to be an ideal master and a strong
disciplinarian who, having rejected koan Zen, stressed
the importance of Zen-sitting. One day during an
early morning zazen session, Nyojo, catching a priest
in the act of dozing off, shouted, "Zen practice aims at
the liberation of body and mind! How can you be dozing?" On hearing these words, Dogen attained satori.
Returning home after five years in China, he lived
first in Kyoto and then near Fukui City, propagating
Zen-sitting pure and simple.

Dogen is the most eminent writer on Zen in Japan.
Both his views on Buddhism and his very profound

Zen dialectics are to be found in the ninety-five essays composing *Shobogenzo* (The Correct-Law Eye Treasury). This work is highly valued not only by Zennists but also by those Japanese philosophers who are more than mere investigators of European ideas.

The following, the shortest essay in *Shobogenzo,* is not only characteristic but gives rather completely Dogen's views on life and death, the fundamental concern of Zen.

On Life and Death

"Since there is Buddhahood in both life and death," says Kassan, "neither exists." Jozan says, "Since there is no Buddhahood in life or death, one is not led astray by either." So go the sayings of the enlightened masters, and he who wishes to free himself of the life-and-death bondage must grasp their seemingly contradictory sense.

To seek Buddhahood outside of life and death is to ride north to reach Southern Etsu or face south to glimpse the North Star. Not only are you traveling the wrong way on the road to emancipation, you are increasing the links in your karma-chain. To find release you must begin to regard life and death as identical to nirvana, neither loathing the former nor coveting the latter.

It is fallacious to think that you simply move from birth to death. Birth, from the Buddhist point of view, is a temporary point between the preceding and the succeeding; hence it can be called birthlessness. The same holds for death and deathlessness. In life there is nothing more than life, in death nothing more than death: we are being born and are dying at every moment.

Now, to conduct: in life identify yourself with life, at death with death. Abstain from yielding and craving. Life and death constitute the very being of Buddha. Thus, should you renounce life and death, you will lose; and you can expect no more if you cling to either. You must neither loathe, then, nor covet, neither think nor speak of these things. Forgetting body and mind, by placing them together in Buddha's hands and letting him lead you on, you will without design or effort gain freedom, attain Buddhahood.

There is an easy road to Buddhahood: avoid evil, do nothing about life-and-death, be merciful to all sentient things, respect superiors and sympathize with inferiors, have neither likes nor dislikes, and dismiss idle thoughts and worries. Only then will you become a Buddha.

II. KEIZAN (1268–1325, Soto)

While Dogen, author of the preceding essay, is revered as Koso (high patriarch), Keizan is honored as Taiso (great patriarch) of the Soto sect. Keizan took holy orders when he was twelve; at the age of twenty-one, while reading in the Saddharma Pundrika Sutra, "The parent-begotten eye sees all the great chiliads," he experienced what he thought was satori. His master, Tettsu, rejected his reading of the sentence as immature. After seven more years of very close application, he succeeded in attaining a genuine awakening. This experience he expressed in the famous utterance, "A pitch-black ball flies through the night." When asked by Tettsu to put it in another way, he said, "I drink tea at teatime, eat rice at mealtime," and this received the master's approval.

Keizan became abbot at several temples, and founded the Soji Temple at Noto in Ishikawa Prefecture (the temple was to be removed to Yokohama), one of the two most important Soto temples in Japan, the other being Eihei. The master wrote several works, the most popular being *Zazen-vojinki* (Directions on Zen Sitting), which should be read by all interested in the subject. *Denkoroku* is a compilation by disciples of his lectures on Buddha and his followers, and on Zen patriarchs. He describes their lives, their attainment of enlightenment, and the manner in which they transmitted the Lamp of Law. The talks are full of great insight, and some of the best of them have been brought together in a series of "sayings" under the title "Excerpts from the Teachings of the Founder of Soji." Our translation, free at times, is from this work; our source is the Rev. Kuruma-Takudo's *Zen-shu-seiten* (Sacred Book of the Zen Sect).

1. *Awakening of the Bodhi-mind (satori)*

It should be clear to all that the Buddhas and patriarchs have never *gained* satori. It is equally true that no ignorant person has ever *gone* astray. Whether awakened or not, one is free. In the awakening of the Bodhi-mind there is neither beginning nor end; while in this mind there is no scale of worth: Buddha and sensual man are as one, being freely and unconditionally just as they are. For numberless kalpas they have followed an unrestrained course, ever conscious of their *karma* (law of cause and effect, or the retributions and rewards earned by one's actions).

2. *The Bonze in Spirit*

To enter the priesthood in spirit is to remain a layman in the midst of worldly cares, hair long, wearing layman's clothes, and most important, it is to remain oneself, as a lotus, undefiled, gem-clear. In this state you will look upon nirvana and life-and-death as floating visionary flowers, and you will rise above passion and enlightenment. Only then will you be possessed of the true spirit of the bonze.

3. *The Ordinary and the Buddhist Dharmas*

Ignoring both the ordinary and the Buddhist dharmas, taking a further view, you will free yourself of doubt and avoid the inward/outward duality or the need of pacification of mind/body.

4. *The Buddhist Truth Permeating the Universe*

The truth taught by Sakyamuni permeates the universe, but only by denying the senses, by avoiding dualistic thoughts, and by minute observation can you hope to attain it. Yet you must not proceed step by step. Rather you must exert yourself once and for all. Only then will you push through to enlightenment.

5. Transformation of Illusion into Satori

What is there to be enlightened about? Only the man of no-satori thinks that illusion can be turned into satori, the profane into the sacred. What illusion is there to awake from, what profane thought to crush?

6. The True Destination of All

The many disciplinary devices of Buddhas and patriarchs offer the way to transcend front/back, up/down, self/others. The emptiness of non-emptiness is the true destination of all. Even if you should negate all till you arrive at all-emptiness, there will remain that which cannot be annihilated.

7. Attainment of Buddha-wisdom

Should you desire to attain Buddha-wisdom quickly, you must free yourself not only from the four inverted beliefs (Hinayanistic beliefs, i.e., all phenomena are impermanent, suffering, impersonal, impure) and the three passions (greed, anger, ignorance), but also from the threefold body (the essential, the glorified, and the revealed Buddha) and the four forms of supreme wisdom (the great mirror, the universal and the profound observation, and the perfecting wisdom). In this state you will be neither a Buddha nor an ordinary man. You will rise above the conceptual area of the profane and the sacred, and move out of reach of arguments based on differentiation.

44

8. *Gaining of Buddhahood and the Way*

Do not be fooled into believing that Buddhahood and the Way can be gained by merit, good works, eating but one meal a day, meditating for long periods, adoring the Buddhas, reciting sutras, etc. All these things amount to planting flowers in the air while digging holes in the earth. Numberless kalpas of such actions will not lead to satori. Not to have any desire whatsoever—that is the Way.

9. *Body and Mind Brought into Being*

You must understand that One exists who is without not only speech but mouth itself, who lacks eyes, the four elements and the six roots of perception [in Buddhism the mind is a sixth sense]. Yet none can call him a void, for it is he alone that brought your body and mind into being.

10. *Body and Mind Are One*

To see the body is to see the mind, to know the mind is to grasp the body: they are identical. Appearing, they do not add a jot; disappearing, not a particle is lost. The four combined elements created your body, while the destruction of all phenomena results in the mind. To understand the Way and realize the mind, one does not have to seek afar.

11. *Body and Mind Indivisible*

Since body and mind are indivisible, so are past and present. Hence the saying, "Nowhere to be born, nowhere to die." Coming and going at their appointed times, beings do not alter the four elements or re-form the five aggregates (form, perception, consciousness, action, knowledge).

12. *Two Bodies, One Mind*

Birth cannot alter the mind, embodiment cannot transmute Original Nature. Though the essential and the physical bodies have changed, mind is as it has always been. And thus it has been for limitless kalpas.

13. *The Mind and the World Are One*

It is as incorrect to say that mind and world are one as it is to say that they are changeless. To hold that words and all reasoning are useless is equally wrong. Can one say that the nature of the self is true and the mind real?

14. *The Sense Organs and Their Fields Both Forgotten*

There are no sense organs to grasp, and there is no need to obliterate their fields. Each is transcended along with the mind and the objective world. Viewed minutely, none has true existence. Reach this state of awareness, and you are ready to inherit the Dharma-store, join the Buddhas and patriarchs.

15. *The Mind Is Formless*

Having no form and in spite of hearing, seeing, knowing, perceiving, the mind is above coming, going, moving, remaining. When you can see it in this way, you are beginning to understand the nature of mind. Yet even then you are no better than a Sravaka ["hearers" still in the initial stage].

16. The Mind Bright and Clear

When all discrimination is abandoned, when contact with things is broken, the mind is brighter than sun and moon together, cleaner than frost and snow.

17. The Mind Originally Pure

Originally pure, the mind is in perfect accord with all it contemplates. Should it turn away from one such object, illusion results. Should the illusion be apprehended, however, the mind regains its purity and one's nature is ethereal once again. Understanding this much, ignorance is overcome along with the twelve links in the chain of existence (the first link, ignorance, leads to the last, death), the four forms of birth (womb-birth, the egg, the grub, the sudden transformation to angel), and the six directions of reincarnation (hells, animals, malevolent spirits and those of nature, humans, and deities). Each of you possesses the Original Mind.

18. The Original Mind Grasped

Once grasped, the Original Mind frees one of the concepts of birth/death, illusion/enlightenment. The four elements, the five aggregates, the triple world (sensuous desire, form, pure spirit), and the six directions of reincarnation are identical hills of beans.

19. The Original Mind Defined

Non-existent are birth, death, nirvana, passions, enlightenment, as they have been from kalpa to kalpa. The truth is—and were it acknowledged as such—that you have always been free of these things, each of you.

20. The Psychic and the Original Mind

The psychic can be divided into the discerning, the perceiving, and the mind. The first is what distinguishes between hatred and love, good and bad. The second is what feels cold and warmth, pain and comfort. The third, like a tree or stone or wall, neither distinguishes nor feels. Neither speech nor thought itself, touches it. Such is the mind, and discernment and perception must be seen as originating within it. Therefore it should not be taken as the Original Mind.

21. Nothing Apart from the Mind

Nothing reveals itself apart from the mind, no dust tarnishes the spirit. Each is above the senses and their objects, each follows the Way, possesses the mind.

22. No Mind Apart from the Body

One's mind has absolute identity with one's self, and one is the Way itself. One must not seek after the formed or formless Buddhas. The body's meaning is this: there is nothing separable. The mind's: there is nothing inseparable. Should one reach this stage, one must not search for mind apart from body.

23. The Mind Transmitted by the Mind

Buddhas follow one upon the other, and so do the patriarchs. In this way mind is transmitted.

24. Being Full One with the Way

Should you desire the true Way, cut loose from egotism, attachments, insolence and pride. Your passion to attain Buddha-wisdom will be as fire joining fire.

25. *Consummate Satori Is Everything*

Even if well-versed in theory and enlightened in the Way, you are wandering until you have gained satori, which is like the Emperor's seal on goods, proof that they are neither contraband nor poisonous.

26. *After Satori, Teach*

Though there is nothing to give or receive, satori should be as conclusive as knowing your face by touching the nose. After gaining satori, teach. Otherwise you will be no better than goblins clinging to grasses and trees. Above all, scorn the heretic's view that things are sufficient to themselves.

27. *Buddha's Proper Teaching*

Should a master tell you that there is a dharma to grasp, should a tempter declare that there is no further dharma to discipline yourself in, do not be disturbed. In order to attain the desired self-tranquilization, learn from Buddhas, and thus gain insight into the truth.

28. *The Way of Tranquilization*

Since the arrival of the Patriarch of the West (Bodhidharma) in China, all—learned/ignorant, tyro/priest —have been taught to practice zazen and to remain in possession of themselves. This is the way of perfect tranquilization.

29. *The Lamp Transmitted by Buddhas and Patriarchs*

The Lamp of Dharma has been transmitted by Buddhas and patriarchs. Holding it up cautiously, train yourself in serenity. But always remember that your Original Mind, calm and lucid, awaits discovery.

30. *The Peerless Grand-Dharma*

Though you apprehend your Original Nature and achieve emancipation as complete as that of the Buddhas and patriarchs, there remains the peerless treasure of Grand-Dharma to give pious ear to. Examine it minutely, you monks, and resolve to be its worthy bearers. In this way you will be touching the warm flesh of Sakyamuni.

III. Muso (1275–1351, Rinzai)

Muso, who was to become National Teacher and first abbot of the famed Tenryu Temple in Kyoto, asked the master Issan to tell him what the Truth was, but the master would not do so. When he went to Koho and told him how Issan had treated him, Koho said, "Well, why didn't you accuse him of being a good-for-nothing?" Of course this did not satisfy Muso, nor answer his original question, so he devoted himself to Zen-sitting all the more seriously. One night, after hours of zazen, he felt exhausted and, on getting up, staggered and fell. At that very moment he gained supreme satori. Though he desired to live as a recluse, his learning and high virtue attracted the Emperor and other dignitaries, and he was forced to remain in the capital and other large cities. For a whole month before his death, he gave "farewell interviews" and his numerous followers came to him for final instructions. Of all his writings, *Muchumondo* (Dream Dialogues), from which the following excerpts have been taken, is the most popular. The work is a simple though very telling commentary on those subjects most important to Zen.

Dream Dialogue

A: When we see suffering we are moved to pity. Why is such sympathy rejected as mercy arising from attachment? Furthermore, if you look upon all sentient beings as nothing more than phantoms, how can you pity them?

B: Well, let's take beggars as an example. They can be divided into two classes: those who, born of beggar parents, have always been in a lowly position, and those who, born of noble parents, have later sunk in fortune.

Naturally you are likely to pity the latter more. Now, the same applies to the Bodhisattva's mercy. All sentient beings are essentially Buddhas, without the marks of life and death, yet sooner or later they are deluded into thinking of life and death, they dream. The Mahayana Bodhisattva is therefore as much moved by the suffering of other sentient beings as by that of beggars of well-to-do parents. In this he is unlike the Hinayana Bodhisattva who, in considering that all beings are caught up in life and death, shows mercy arising from attachment.

A: Just as a drunkard is not aware of his state, so he who has yielded to Mara's [Devil] temptation is unaware of the fact. Thus he is unable to release himself. How can one resist Mara?

B: Fearing Mara, you are possessed by him. Nagarjuna writes, "If you have mind, you are caught in the Mara-net; without mind, you need not fear it." An old master said, "There are none of Mara's hindrances outside the mind: no mind, no Mara." Master Doju, you'll remember, conquered Mara by neither hearing nor seeing.

To cling to Buddhahood is to be in the Mara-realm; to forget Mara is to be in the Buddha-realm. A true Zennist is neither attached to the Buddha-realm nor fearful of Mara, then, and with fortitude, with no thought of gain, will remain in this state. Also, of course, you must make a vow before Buddha's image. The Perfect Enlightenment Sutra says, "Those living in a corrupt age must make this great vow of purification: May we attain Buddha's perfect enlightenment and, not ruled by non-Buddhists, Sravakas, and Pratyeka-Buddhas [those who gain enlightenment for their own salvation], but under good instruction, surmount obstacles one by one and enter the sanctified place of enlightenment." Aided by this great vow, even a tyro will not be won over to devils and heretics throughout his successive lives. Supported by Buddhas and devas, all impediments removed, such a man will reach the never-receding state of tranquillity.

A: Even if he trains strictly, in accordance with the deep doctrines, it is possible that a beginner be misled. Indeed some masters discourage doctrinal studies while insisting on discipline pure and simple. How would you justify this standpoint?

B: Well, can one who has learned something about medicine cure himself of a serious illness? No. He must go to another for treatment and, without inquiring how it was compounded, take the medicine given him. The same is true of Zen discipline. If the seeker after the fundamental self, which is the aim of satori, tries to learn different doctrines and then, acting upon what he has learned, sets about training himself, he is probably doomed to ignorance. The doctines are so numerous, life so short. At the end of his life he will see all the books and their learning as a heap of trash; dazed, he will be forced by karma along the cycle of rebirth. That is why Zen masters give you but a word or two, and these are not meant to provide a moral lesson but serve as a direct index of your fundamental self. Dull-witted students may not be able to understand the master's words at once, but if they continue to masticate them as a koan beyond the reach of intellect and sensibility, they will sooner or later rid themselves of the most persistent illusion. Suddenly it will be gone to the four winds.

A: Should one cast off worldly feelings—anger, joy, etc.—before applying himself to the examination of the Truth?

B: All humans, because they are able to profit by the Buddha's Law, are fortunate: it is the greatest rarity in the world. Nothing is less to be relied on than life, the inbreathing, the outbreathing. Knowing it for what it is, you must not yield to worldly feelings nor neglect your study of Zen. But suppose an emotion of that kind is felt. Well, you must examine it minutely, just as it has risen. In this way your feelings can actually help you in your training. But the less-than-serious students must be taught differently: they must be helped in the task of alleviation, which does not mean, of course, that they should be told to eliminate all emotion before undertaking Zen discipline. The one important thing is the awakening and, once it has been attained, the ordinary man is a man of satori, however many emotions he retains.

Even when an emotion is felt, you must not give up probing. As you well know, the most religious are often forgetful of eating and sleeping, for even while doing these things they are scrutinizing themselves without obstacle. Though this is not exactly what the less religious are advised to do, they too should of course continue in self-examination. An ancient said, "While walking, examine the walking; while sitting, the sitting, etc." The same holds true of joy and sorrow. An excellent admonition, that, and one likely to lead to an awakening.

A: There is disagreement about the importance of koan, some considering it all-important; others, paltry. What is your view of the matter?

B: It all depends on the master, the koan being but an expedient. There is no fixed rule about its use. A master once asked his pupil, "Are you in full accord with your koan?" When student and koan are as one, there is neither examined nor examiner. To one advanced as

54

far as that, your question is meaningless. The less advanced, however, may properly do the koan exercise. The master alone, of course, can determine the outcome. Anyone without insight who simply reads the words of the old masters and then proceeds to teach his own hidebound opinions behaves in a most dangerous way. An ancient censured just such an instructor as binding others to a Hinayanistic view of entity.

IV. MEIHO (1277–1350, Soto)

Meiho, fifth patriarch of the Japanese Soto sect, spent eight years disciplining himself under Keizan. He gained satori while grappling with the koan, "What is it that makes all things wax and wane?" He then deepened his Zen under other masters, finally returning to Keizan and succeeding him. He scorned all gain and fame, and urged his disciples to devote themselves to Zen-sitting alone. The following sermon is one of the best-known writings on zazen ever done by a Japanese.

Zazen

Zen-sitting is the way of perfect tranquillity: inwardly not a shadow of perception, outwardly not a shade of difference between phenomena. Identified with yourself, you no longer think, nor do you seek enlightenment of the mind or disburdenment of illusions. You are a flying bird with no mind to twitter, a mountain unconscious of the others rising around it.

Zen-sitting has nothing to do with the doctrine of "teaching, practice, and elucidation" or with the exercise of "commandments, contemplation, and wisdom." You are like a fish with no particular design of remaining in the sea. Nor do you bother with sutras or ideas. To control and pacify the mind is the concern of lesser men: Sravakas, Pratyeka-Buddhas, and Hinayanists. Still less can you hold an idea of Buddha and Dharma. If you attempt to do so, if you train improperly, you are like one who, intending to voyage west, moves east. You must not stray.

Also you must guard yourself against the easy conceptions of good and evil: your sole concern should be to examine yourself continually, asking who is above either. You must remember too that the unsullied essence of life has nothing to do with whether one is priest or layman, man or woman. Your Buddha-nature, consummate as the full moon, is represented by your position as you sit in Zen. The exquisite Way of Buddhas is not the One or Two, being or non-being. What diversifies it is the limitations of its students, who can be divided into three classes—superior, average, inferior.

The superior student is unaware of the coming into the world of Buddhas or of the transmission of the non-transmittable by them: he eats when hungry, sleeps when sleepy. Nor does he regard the world as himself. Neither is he attached to enlightenment or illusion. Taking things as they come, he sits in the proper manner, making no idle distinctions.

The average student discards all business and ignores the external, giving himself over to self-examination with every breath. He may probe into a koan, which he puts mentally on the tip of his nose, finding in this way that his "original face" (fundamental being) is beyond life and death, and that the Buddha-nature of all is not dependent on the discriminating intellect but is the unconscious consciousness, the incomprehensible understanding: in short, that it is clear and distinct for all ages and is alone apparent in its entirety throughout the universe.

The inferior student must disconnect himself from all that is external, thus liberating himself from the duality of good and evil. The mind, just as it is, is the origin of all Buddhas. In zazen his legs are crossed so that his Buddha-nature will not be led off by evil thoughts, his hands are linked so that they will not take up sutras or implements, his mouth is shut so that he refrains from preaching a word of *dharma* or uttering blasphemies, his eyes are half shut so that he does not distinguish between objects, his ears are closed to the world so that he will not hear talk of vice and virtue, his nose is as if dead so that he will not smell good or bad. Since his body has nothing on which to lean, he is indifferent to likes and dislikes. He negates neither being nor non-being. He sits like Buddha on the pedestal, and though distorted ideas may arise from him, they do so idly and are ephemeral, constituting no sin, like reflections in a mirror, leaving no trace.

The five, the eight, the two hundred and fifty commandments, the three thousand monastic regulations, the eight hundred duties of the Bodhisattva, the Buddha-nature and the Bodhisattvahood, and the Wheel of Dharma—all are comprised in Zen-sitting and emerge from it. Of all good works, zazen comes first, for the merit of only one step into it surpasses that of erecting a thousand temples. Even a moment of sitting will enable you to free yourself from life and death, and your Buddha-nature will appear of itself. Then all you do, perceive, think becomes part of the miraculous Tathata-suchness (true nature, thusness).

Let it be thus remembered that tyros and advanced students, learned and ignorant, all without exception should practice zazen.

V. JAKUSHITSU (1290–1367, Rinzai)

Founder of the Eigenji School of the Rinzai sect, Jakushitsu had an awakening at eighteen when, at his query, "What is the ultimate word of Truth?", his master, Yakuo, gave him a slap. After working with several other masters, he went to China and remained there seven years, enriching his Zen under important masters. It is said that during his voyage back home a violent storm arose and the ship was about to sink, but, sitting in Zen, Jakushitsu was able to invoke the aid of Avalokitesvara (a Bodhisattva) and the storm subsided. Once back in Japan he led a very secluded life for twenty-five years. His followers built for him the Eigen Temple in Omi Province, and many came to him for guidance. The "warnings" that follow give an idea of how he disciplined them.

Ten Warnings to the Congregation

1. Always bear in mind that life, whose gravest problems are birth and death, is impermanent.

2. In order to avoid violating commandments, govern mind and body.

3. Take care not to adhere to nothingness, nor brag of your industry, nor backslide into the views of the Sravaka-Pratyeka Buddhist.

4. Regulating mind and body, avoiding all illusions, sit fast in Zen.

5. If you would avoid the tenebrous cave of demons, do not mistake mere divine illumination for satori.

6. Do not indulge in eating and sleeping. Spine like an iron bolt, sit night and day in Zen.

7. Scrutinize your Original Face, which had its being long before the birth of your parents.

8. Weigh your koan to the minutest detail, but do not be impatient to gain satori.

9. Rather than spend aeons without an awakening, have no second thoughts.

10. Clearly understanding the Grand Law, be firm in resolution, preserve all Buddha-wisdom.

VI. TETSUO (1295–1369, Rinzai)

Tetsuo, a disciple of the National Teacher Daito, was given by him the koan, "What does having mastery over externals mean?" He presented view after view, but each was rejected by the master. Finally after long meditation, during which he all but forgot food and drink, he had a consummate awakening. He once said to his followers, "This or that: give me the absolute word!" At which a monk came forward and said, "You say it, and at once, master!"

"Why don't you?" said Tetsuo.

The monk slapped the master's face.

Then, grabbing the monk, Tetsuo cried, "You know the gimlet is sharp, all right, but not that the chisel is square!"

"I can't agree to that," said the monk.

Tetsuo spat in his face and thrust him away.

The sermon below expresses well Tetsuo's views on freedom and mastery.

How to Awaken

Most students of Zen apply themselves to mindless zazen—a grave error. It should be remembered that the mind is transmitted and enlightened by itself. The nonsentient cannot attain the Way. Students today can't seem to grasp that to feel cold or warmth, hunger or fullness, is to be mindless and on the right path. For this very reason an ancient Chinese master, Baso, said, "The mind is Buddha," and another Chinese master, Nansen, "The ordinary mind is the Way."

The student should go beyond the feeling of cold or warmth, hunger or fullness, until there is not a shadow of the mind. In this way he will awaken, regain his original being, which arcs serenely as the rainbow. Then he can walk or sit at his own sweet will, led on to mastery over human affairs. That is the living patriarch's way.

VII. Ryoho (1305–1384, Rinzai)

Ryoho had an awakening while training with Ryoshin, then worked with other masters to deepen his Zen. Later he spent three years alone in the mountains, sitting in Zen, and feeding, it is said, on berries dropped him daily by birds. His Zen insight and his literary talent won him fame among the high and low, including Yoshimitsu, the Shogun. His Zen spirit is revealed in these short sermons.

On Emptiness

1. The Buddhas of all times and places preach the empty dharma with their empty bodies, so as to enable empty beings to realize equally empty Buddhahood. For this reason the Buddha declared, "Even if there is something excelling nirvana, it is an empty dream."

If anyone in the reality of "suchness" can understand the dharma of dreamy emptiness and examine and practice it, he will through the dharma of reality conquer self and cherish mercy. In this way he will be able to invent a discipline and devices for what is called "The Way of Purity and Universal Emancipation." If, however, he lingers in this view, he will not be able to attain the proper mental state of the Zen-man.

What is the one phrase (Ryoho lifted his staff before going on) that will lead you to the proper state? Well, say it! (Ryoho's staff came down with a thump.) Don't sleep, and you won't dream!

2. All things being empty, so is the mind. As the mind is empty, all is. My mind is not divisible: all is contained in my every thought, which appears as enlightenment to the wise, illusion to the stupid. Yet en-

lightenment and illusion are one. Do away with both, but don't remain "in between" either. In this way you will be emptiness itself, which, stainless and devoid of the interrelationship of things, transcends realization. In this way the true Zen priest commonly conducts himself.

VIII. SHOZAN (1579–1655, Rinzai)

A samurai until his forty-fifth year, Shozan then took Zen orders and finally was to succeed Gudo. He emphasized what is called Nio-Zen-Sitting, a type of Zen befitting an ex-samurai with a record of distinguished service, and certainly representative of a phase of Japanese Zen. It is said that he scorned the trivialities, even going so far as to eat fish and drink wine, which are normally avoided by Buddhists. The following are from *Roankyo*, a collection of his most important talks.

Nio-Zen

1. A man said to the master, "Of course, I never think of death." To which the master responded, "That's all very well, but you'll not get very far in Zen, I'm afraid. As for myself, well, I train in Zen in detestation of death and in hope of deathlessness, and I am resolved to carry on in this way, from life to life, until I realize my aim. That you do not think of death shows that you are not a man of enlightenment, because you are incapable of knowing your master, whatever there is in you that uses the six sense organs."

2. In studying Zen you should take Buddha images for models, but that of Tathagata (the Buddha in his corporeal manifestation) does not suit the beginner, because the Tathagata type of zazen is beyond him. Rather model yourself on images of Nio [Vajrapani: literally "Diamond Deity," an indomitable guardian of Buddhism of ferocious mien] and Fudo, both of which are symbolic of discipline. This is apparent from the fact that Nios stand in temple gates, and Fudo is the

first of the thirteen Buddhas. Without spirit and vigor you'll be passion's slave. Like these deities, have a dauntless mind.

Unfortunately Buddhism has declined, going from bad to worse, with the result that most are milksops, critically lacking in vigor. Only the valorous can train properly, the ignorant being mild and sanctimonious, mistaken in the belief that such is the way of Buddhist practice. Then there are the madmen who go about trumpeting their attainment of satori—a bagatelle. Myself, I'm a stranger to sanctimoniousness and satorishness, my sole aim being to conquer all with a vivacious mind. Sharing the vitality of Nio and Fudo, exterminate all of your evil karma and passions. (Here the master paused, eyes set, hands clenched, teeth gnashing.) Guard yourself closely, and nothing will be able to interfere. Only bravery will carry you through. We'll have no part of weaklings here! Be wide awake, and attain the vigor of living Zen.

3. The master once gave the following instructions to a samurai: "You had better practice zazen while busily occupied. The samurai's zazen must be the sort that will support him in the midst of battle, when he is threatened by guns and spears. After all, what use can the tranquilizing type of sitting be on the battlefield? You should foster the Nio spirit above all. All worldly arts are cultivated through Zen-sitting. The military arts especially cannot be practiced with a feeble spirit. (So saying, the master pretended to draw a sword.) Zazen must be virile, yet the warrior upholds it only in battle; no sooner does he sheathe his sword than he's off guard again. The Buddhist, on the other hand, always maintains vigor. Never is he a loser. The more he

ripens in discipline, the more adept he becomes in everything, from the recitation of a text to tapping a hand drum in Noh. Perfect in all virtues, he can fit in anywhere."

4. A priest asked the master, "Are not your works such as *Fumotokusawake* based on a notion of relative reality?"

"Of course," said the master. "But you know the common man's mind is without exception one of relative reality. And how can you undergo Zen training without such a mind? Many masters nowadays lapse into notions of nothingness, leading their followers astray. They reside complacently in what they call original vacuity, which is the relative reality you speak of. Generally speaking, if you seek satori with your mind, you will leave behind the notion of being. However, if you cling with your no-mind to original vacuity, you cannot hope to succeed. Honen (1133–1212), founder of the Jodo [Pure Land] sect, for example, invoked Amitabha Buddha not with the no-mind but with the mind. And if you try to picture the Pure Land as really existing and repeat Amitabha's name, you will gain the virtue of no-mind. On the other hand, those who now pose as exponents of the primary void, and reject Zen discipline as something concerned with relative being, are merely accumulating evil karma.

5. A birdcatcher: "We have always been birdcatchers. If we give up, we'll starve. While following this trade, is it possible for me to attain Buddhahood?"

Master: "The mind falls into hell, not the body. Each time you kill a bird, grasp your mind and kill it also. In this way you can attain Buddhahood."

6. The master cheered up an eighteen-year-old monk on the point of death by saying: "However long one lives, life goes on unchanging. You are lucky if you can discard the body, a thing of filth and suffering, even a single day earlier than others. In any case, you'll be free of life's bondage. I have lived to this old age without having seen one new thing. You may think Master Dogen a free man, but not so. He fell short of Lord Buddha's enlightenment, which is beyond the power of all of us. You know, many have failed in achieving their ends, not you alone. Even a long life can be flat, after all. The best thing is to cast the foul body aside as soon as possible. I promise to follow you soon."

On hearing the master's words, the monk passed away in the proper frame of mind.

IX. MANZAN (1635–1714, Soto)

Manzan expressed his spiritual attainment with the following: "Even in a single thought unborn, the All is apparent." This insight was approved by his master, Gesshu. It is to his credit that, along with Baiho, he succeeded in reforming the lax views of lineage and succession that had plagued his sect for a hundred years. The *Manzan-koroku* is a compilation of his sayings and writings.

Letter to Zissan
[Zissan: a monk's name, suggesting "real practice."]

Like training, satori must be true. If one holds that there is something to practice and realize, one is a follower of the false religion of entity based on affirmation. If, on the other hand, one asserts that there is nothing to practice or realize, one is still not above the four types of differentiation and the one hundred forms of negation: one is an adherent of the equally false religion of nothingness, founded on negation. And this is the shadowy product of the dichotomous intellect, holding no truth.

First of all, I ask you to look upon the world's riches as a dunghill, upon the most beautiful men and women as stinking corpses, upon the highest honors and reputation as an echo, upon the most malicious calumny as the cawing of a crow. Regard yourself as a fan in winter, the universe as a straw dog.

This accomplished, train wholeheartedly. Then, and only then, will you awaken. If you dare claim to have undergone real training and attained enlightenment without having gone through all this, you are nothing but a liar and are bound for hell. Bear all I have said in mind—practice truly.

X. TAKUSUI (17th–18th centuries, Rinzai)

Takusui trained under Kian, eventually became his successor. It is recorded that he attained an awakening only after long study of the directions for Zen training given in *Bassui's Sermons*, as is apparent from the following sermons. A kindly and ingenuous master, Takusui trained disciples in Edo (the old name of Tokyo), and is said to have lived for more than one hundred and sixty years.

1. If you desire the attainment of satori, ask yourself this question: Who hears sound? As described in the Surangama-samadhi, that is Avalokitesvara's faith in the hearer. Since there is such a hearer in you, all of you hear sounds. You may say that it is the ear that hears, yet the ear is but a mechanism. If it could hear by itself, then the dead could hear our prayers for them. Inside you, then, is a hearer.

Now, this is the way to apply yourself: whether or not you hear anything, keep asking who the hearer is. Doubt, scrutinize, paying no attention to fancies or ideas. Strain every nerve without expecting anything to happen, without willing satori. Doubt, doubt, doubt. If even one idea arises, your doubt is not sufficiently strong, and you must question yourself more intensely. Scrutinize the hearer in yourself, who is beyond your power or vision.

Master Bassui says, "When at wits' end and unable to think another thought, you are applying yourself properly." Thus do not look around, but devote yourself utterly to doubting self-examination until you forget where you are or even that you live. This may lead you to feel completely at sea. Yet you must persist in the search for the hearer, sweating, like a dead man, until you are unconscious, a lump of great doubt. But look! That lump will suddenly break up and out of it will leap the angel of the awakening, the great satori consciousness. It is as if one awoke from the deepest dream, literally returned to life.

2. In Zen practice a variety of supernatural phenomena may be experienced. For example, you may see ghostly faces, demons, Buddhas, flowers, or you may feel your body becoming like that of a woman, or even purified into a state of non-existence. If this happens, your "doubt in practice" is still inadequate, for if in perfect doubt you will not have such illusions. Indeed it is only when you are not alert that you meet with them. Do not shrink from them, nor prize them. Just doubt and examine yourself all the more thoroughly.

3. Zen practitioners must accept the fact that while in meditation they are likely to suffer one or more of the three maladies: *kon*, *san*, and *chin*. *Kon* is sleepiness and *san* instability, both of which are too well known for comment. *Chin*, on the other hand, is a grave malady and always leads to unhappy results. It is a state in which one is free from sleepiness and instability, and all mentalization ceases. One feels gay, immaculate; one can go on in zazen for hours on end. One has a feeling that all things are equal, neither existent nor non-existent, right nor wrong. Those possessed by chin regard it as satori—a most dangerous delusion. If you were to remain in this state, you would go far astray. At such times, in fact, you must have the greatest doubt.

XI. BANKEI-EITAKU (1622–1693, Rinzai)

The two most important masters in the history of Japanese Zen are Dogen (1200–1253) and Hakuin (1685–1768). Dogen introduced from China the Soto sect, which still flourishes and is one of the two most important sects today, and wrote *Shobogenzo*, a collection of essays on Zen treasured as the Bible of his sect; Hakuin restored single-handed the then declining Rinzai sect and, by creating a remarkable system of koan, which is followed by all disciplinarians of the sect, established a solid basis for its continuance. It is assumed that these masters, selections of whose work can be found elsewhere in this volume, are familiar to all interested in Zen.

Bankei is a master who represents a very special phase of Japanese Zen. As proof of the profound respect in which he is held, mention might be made of the publication in 1942 of *Studies in Bankei Zen*, a compilation of nine essays by the editors, Dr. Suzuki, Professor Furuta, and other contributors, in commemoration of the two hundred and fiftieth anniversary of the master's death. In the essay that opens the book, Dr. Suzuki says: ". . . in the whole history of Zen, both in China and Japan, there is none, it may be said, who has displayed so independent a view as Bankei."

If we were asked to characterize in a few words these three masters, we might venture the following: Dogen is a wonderfully profound dialectician, Hakuin a robust poet and Bankei an intuitionist, pure and simple.

It was only after years of truly desperate effort that Bankei succeeded in gaining satori, perhaps the most thorough and pregnant of its kind. He called what he had grasped the "birthless Buddha-mind," and preached it tirelessly and with the utmost generosity to the end of his life. His language was so plain and direct that even the unlettered among his auditors were able to understand him. A regular priest, he served as superior at a number of Zen temples, among them the famous Myoshinji in Kyoto. Yet he was too great to limit or bind himself to what was called the Zen sect, in his eyes a stereotyped form. He considered himself to be the birthless Buddha-mind itself, and wanted to share his secret, which was no less than a penetration into the very truth of life, with others.

What follows is a free and selective rendering of the first fifty-six pages of Bankei-zenji's *Sayings and Writings*, compiled and edited by Dr. Suzuki as one of the volumes of the Iwanami Library. The order of the talks does not always follow the original. It should be made clear that the talks were recorded by a disciple in the colloquial Japanese of three hundred years ago, and it is evident that he wanted above all to preserve as accurately as possible the master's words.

(A word of caution. As will be clear to the reader, Bankei was above the use of special devices in making people achieve the satori of the birthless Buddha-mind. He simply preached and exhorted. Indeed this may be the feature that appeals to common people, and yet it presents a grave problem from the standpoint of practical Zen. Being an uncommon man, Bankei was able to influence many, but after his death, his type of Zen had, by its very nature, to die out: he wanted people to attain satori without effort, but it is an iron law of Zen that great effort be made, the sort of effort that Bankei himself had to make. Dogen insisted on the importance of sitting in Zen, Hakuin employed the koan systematically, and so on.)

The Zen of Birthlessness

1.

How lucky you are these days! When I was young there wasn't a good master to be found. At least I couldn't uncover one. But the truth is I was rather simple when young, and made one blunder after another. And the fruitless efforts! I don't suppose I'll ever forget those days, if only because they were so painful. That's why I come here every day. I want to teach you how to avoid the blunders I made. How lucky you are these days!

I'm going to tell you about some of my mistakes, and I know you're clever enough—every one of you—to learn from what I say. If by chance one of you should be led astray by my example, the sin will be unpardonable. That must be avoided at all costs. Indeed it was only after great hesitation that I decided to tell you of my experiences. Remember then, you can learn from me without imitating.

My parents came here from the island of Shikoku, and it was right here [the province of Harima in Hyogo Prefecture] that I was born. My father was a lordless samurai and a Confucian scholar as well, but he died when I was a child and I was brought up by my mother. She was to tell me later that I was boss of all the children in the neighborhood (which led me to do a lot of mischief) and that roughly from my third year I began to loathe death, so much so in fact that when I cried all she had to do was mimic a corpse, or even say "death," and I'd stop crying and become good.

When yet a small boy I became interested in Confucianism, which in those days was very popular. One day while reading *Great Learning* [a classic of Chinese philosophy] I came upon the sentence, "The path of the Great Learning lies in clarifying illustrious virtue." This was completely beyond me, and I wondered about illustrious virtue for days on end, asking teacher after teacher, but to no avail. Finally one of them took me aside and said, "Go to a Zen priest. They know all about difficult things of this kind. All we do, day in, day out, is explain the meaning of the Chinese characters and, of course, lecture a bit. We know nothing about your 'illustrious virtue,' I'm afraid. Go ask a Zen priest, I tell you."

I'd have been happy to follow his advice, but there were no Zen priests around at the time. One of the chief motives for my wanting to know about illustrious virtue was that I felt duty bound to teach my mother the path of the Great Learning before she died. I kept going to hear all the Confucian and Buddhist lectures, and would return to her with the wisdom that had been imparted to me, but, alas, my questions remained unanswered.

One day I remembered a certain Zen master and went to him full of expectation. At once I asked him about illustrious virtue. He looked at me gravely and said that to understand I would have to sit in Zen meditation. Soon I would be able to grasp it. Well, I lost no time. Often I would go into the mountains and sit in Zen without taking a morsel for a week, or I would go to a rocky place and, choosing the sharpest rock, meditate for days on end, taking no food, until I toppled over. The results? Exhaustion, a shrunken stomach, and an increased desire to go on.

I returned to my village and entered a hermitage, where sleeping in an upright position and living arduously, I gave myself up to the old spiritual exercise of repeating the name of Amitabha. The results? More exhaustion, and huge painful sores on my bottom. It was impossible for me to sit in comfort, but in those days I was pretty tough. Nevertheless to ease the pain, I had to place layers of soft paper under me, which as they lost their effectiveness had constantly to be replaced. Sometimes I was forced to use cotton, so atrocious was the pain.

I knew I was overdoing it, of course, and finally I became seriously ill. Soon I was bringing up blood, lumps the size of a thumb end. One day I spat on the wall and watched fascinated as the lump of blood rolled down. I was in bad shape, I can tell you. On the advice of friends I engaged a servant to nurse me. Once for seven days running I could eat nothing but a gruel of thin rice. I felt my time was up and kept saying to myself, "No help for it. Soon I'll die without obtaining my old desire."

Suddenly, while at the very depths, it struck me like a thunderbolt that *I had never been born*, and that my birthlessness could settle any and every matter. This seemed to be my satori, the awakening I had been waiting for. I realized then that because I'd been ignorant of this simple truth, I'd suffered needlessly.

I began to feel better, and my appetite returned. I called my servant over and said, "I want a big bowl of rice. Right now." He looked puzzled, for he'd been expecting me to keel over; then he set about in a flurry to prepare the meal. In fact he made it so quickly, and in such a state, that the rice was only half-done and stiff. But I ate three bowls and, I can assure you, it didn't disagree with me. Daily my health improved, and soon I was able to accomplish the greatest desire of my life: I was able to get my mother to see the truth, the secret of birthlessness, before she died.

What I wanted now was the "certification" of my satori. My teacher of Confucianism mentioned a Zen priest by the name of Gudo in the province of Mino who would be able to say whether my experience was genuine. I went to Mino in search of him, but unfortunately he had left a few days before for Tokyo. Not wanting the journey to be a waste of time, I called on some Zen priests of Mino and asked if they would aid me. Immediately they complied by giving me their idea of true Zen. I listened carefully, then said, "Please pardon my impudence, but I want to say something. Your opinions are good as far as they go, but frankly you don't go deep enough. At any rate, I'm not satisfied."

At this their spokesman, who had impressed me as an honest and humble man, said, "You're right, I'm afraid. All we do is merely memorize the sutras and some of the Zen writings, then repeat them like parrots to anyone who will listen. I'm afraid none of us has experienced satori, in spite of knowing that a man who has not done so will never hit the mark. We really envy you."

I thanked them and returned home where I kept to myself most of the time and observed how teachable men were, and I weighed the manner in which I could best help them. One day I chanced to learn that a Zen master, Doja, had come to Nagasaki from China. He would be just the man to be my witness, I thought, and straightaway I went to him and told him of my awakening, which had enabled me to virtually transcend life and death. He assured me that I had experienced the real thing and ended up by congratulating me. Naturally I was very pleased, and very grateful to him.

Now it was my turn to begin helping others, and I have been doing just that ever since. That's why I come here to talk to you. It is my desire to bear witness to your satori. You must feel that you are favored. Come forward and let me know if you have had an awakening, and those of you who haven't had the experience, listen carefully to my words. It's in each of you to utterly change your life!

The birthless Buddha-mind can cut any and every knot. You see, the Buddhas of the past, present and future, and all successive patriarchs should be thought of as mere names for what has been born. From the viewpoint of birthlessness, they are of little significance. To live in a state of non-birth is to attain Buddhahood; it is to keep your whereabouts unknown not only to people but even to Buddhas and patriarchs. A blessed state. From the moment you have begun to realize this fact, you are a living Buddha, and need make no further efforts on your *tatami* mats.

Once you begin to understand this you will be unerring in your judgment of others. These days my eye never sizes up a man incorrectly, and each of you possesses the birthless eye. That's why we call our sect the True-eye as well as the Buddha-mind sect. You must not consider yourselves enlightened Buddhas, of course, until you are able to see into others' minds with your birthless eyes. I suppose you may think what I say doubtful, but the moment you have awakened you'll be able to penetrate the minds of others. To prepare you for this is my greatest desire.

I never lie. I could not deceive you. The doctrine of birthlessness died out long ago in China and Japan, but it's now being revived—by me. When you have fully settled in the immaculate Buddha-mind of non-birth, nothing will deceive you, no one will be able to persuade you a crow is a heron. When you've achieved the final enlightenment, you'll be sure of the truth at all times. Nothing, I repeat, no one, will be able to deceive you.

When as a young bonze I began preaching birthlessness there wasn't anyone around who could understand. They were frightened, and they must have thought me a heretic, as bad as a Roman Catholic. Not a single person dared approach me. But gradually they began to see their mistake, and today all you have to do is look around you to see how many come to me. Why, I've hardly any time for myself! Everything in its season, I guess.

In the forty years I've lived here I've instructed many like yourselves, and I've no hesitation in claiming that some of these people are as good in every way as the Zen masters themselves.

2.

The mind begotten by and given to each of us by our parents is none other than the Buddha-mind, birthless and immaculate, sufficient to manage all that life throws up to us. A proof: suppose at this very instant, while you face me listening, a crow caws and a sparrow twitters somewhere behind you. Without any intention on your part of distinguishing between these sounds, you hear each distinctly. In so doing you are hearing with the birthless mind, which is yours for all eternity.

Well, we are to be in this mind from now on, and our sect will be known as the Buddha-mind sect. To consider, once again, my example of a moment ago, if any of you feel you heard the crow and the sparrow intentionally, you are deluding yourselves, for you are listening to me, not to what goes on behind you. In spite of this there are moments when you hear such sounds distinctly, when you hear with the Buddha-mind of non-birth. This nobody here can deny. All of you are living Buddhas, because the birthless mind which you possess is the beginning and the basis of all.

Now, if the Buddha-mind is birthless, it is necessarily immortal, for how can what has never been born perish? You've all encountered the phrase "birthless and imperishable" in the sutras, but until now you've not had the slightest proof of its truth. Indeed I suppose like most people you've memorized this phrase while being ignorant of birthlessness.

When I was twenty-five I realized that non-birth is all-sufficient to life, and since then, for forty years, I've been proving it to people just like you. I was the first to preach this greatest truth of life. I ask you, have any of you priests heard anyone else teach this truth before me? Of course not.

3.
A certain priest once said to me, "You teach the same thing over and over again. Wouldn't it be a good idea, just for the sake of variety, to tell some of those old and interesting stories illustrative of Buddhist life?"

I may be nothing more than an old dunce, and I suppose it might help some if I did tell stories of that kind, but I've a strong hunch that such preaching poisons the mind. No, I would never carry on in so harmful a way. Indeed I make it a rule not to give even the words of Buddha himself, let alone the Zen patriarchs.

To attain the truth today all one needs is self-criticism. There's no need to talk about Buddhism and Zen. Why, there's not a single straying person among you:

all of you have the Buddha-mind. If one of you thinks himself astray, let him come forward and show me in what way. I repeat: there's no such man here.

However, suppose on returning home you were to see one of your children or a servant doing something offensive, and at once you got yourself involved, went astray, turning the Buddha-mind into a demon's, so to speak. But remember, until that moment you were secure in the birthless Buddha-mind. Only at that moment, only then were you deluded.

Don't get involved! Don't get involved with anyone, whoever he happens to be; rather by ridding yourself of the need for others (which really is a form of self-love) remain in the Buddha-mind. Then you will never stray, then you will be a living Buddha for all time.

4.

PRIEST: I was born with a quick temper and, in spite of my master's constant admonitions, I haven't been able to rid myself of it. I know it's a vice, but, as I said, I was born with it. Can you help me?

BANKEI: My, what an interesting thing you were born with! Tell me, is your temper quick at this very moment? If so, show me right off, and I'll cure you of it.

PRIEST: But I don't have it at this moment.

BANKEI: Then you weren't born with it. If you were, you'd have it at all times. You lose your temper as occasion arises. Else where can this hot temper possibly be? Your mistake is one of self-love, which makes you concern yourself with others and insists that you have your own way. To say you were born a hothead is to tax your parents with something that is no fault of theirs. From them you received the Buddha-mind, nothing else.

This is equally true of other types of illusion. If you don't fabricate illusions, none will disturb you. Certainly you were born with none. Only your selfishness and deplorable mental habits bring them into being. Yet you think of them as inborn, and in everything you do, you continue to stray. To appreciate the pricelessness of the Buddha-mind, and to steer clear of illusion, is the one path to satori and Buddhahood.

It is essential that you not yield to quick temper, for to yield and then to try to cure it is to double the burden. Mark well how you stand. Indeed you're in a rather fortunate position, for once rid of hot temper, it will be easy for you to strip yourself of other illusions. Remain firmly in the self-sufficient Buddha-mind of non-birth.

My advice, then, is that you accustom yourself to remaining in a state of non-birth. Try it for thirty days, and you'll be incapable of straying from it: you'll live in the Buddha-mind for the rest of your life. Be reborn this very day! You can be if you give your ear to me, and forget as so much rubbish all your preconceptions. Indeed at my one word of exhortation, you can gain satori.

5.

Hearing Bankei talk in this way, a layman from the province of Izumo said, "If your teaching is right, one should be able to feel at ease in the Buddha-mind at all times, but frankly it all seems a bit weightless."

BANKEI: By no means! Those who make light of the Buddha-mind transform it when angry into a demon's, into a hungry ghost's when greedy, into an animal's when acting stupidly. I tell you my teaching is far from frivolous! Nothing can be so weighty as the Buddha-

Plate 1. Landscape scroll by Kano Minenobu (1662-1708), second son of Tsunenobu. The painter founded a new family of painters, the Hamacho Family. Orv Joyner, Regional Services, Northern Illinois University.

Plate 2. Scroll of Eggplants, typical of tea ceremony scrolls, by Tsurusawa Tanzan (1655-1729). Eggplants are symbolic of good luck. The painter was the first of Kano Tan-yu's four great disciples. The border and backing signify that it was made for a lord of the Tokugawa Period (1600-1868). Orv Joyner, Regional Services, Northern Illinois University.

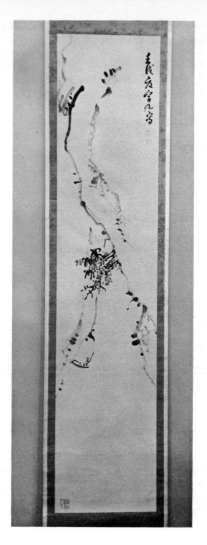

Plate 3. Narrow scroll of Boatman by I Fu-chiu, Chinese painter of the Nan-ga or Southern School, who worked in Nagasaki from 1720 and is said to have been one of Ike-no Taiga's teachers. Certainly I Fu-chiu was a great influence on Taiga, whose "Plum Blossom" is used on the cover of this volume. Orv Joyner, Regional Services, Northern Illinois University.

Sengai (1750-1837, Rinzai), five of whose scroll paintings follow, and who is represented in the text (see the poem by him and Anecdotes 7 and 8), is one of the most famous Zen artists and poets. He was also an outstanding master who served for thirty years as abbot of the Seifukuji in Fukuoka Prefecture. He used to say of his paintings, "My paintings observe no law, but they have law within lawlessness." Speaking of the impact of exhibitions of his paintings on European artists, Herbert Read said, "Sengai came to Europe and has shown the way out of the present *impasse* in art." (Reproduced by courtesy of Idemitsu Kosan Co., Ltd., Japan.)

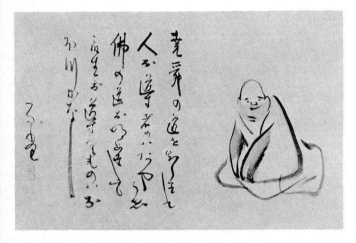

Plate 4. To the Monks

As it is dangerous to be led by those who are ignorant of the Way of Gyo and Shin (two Chinese sage-kings), so it is with those who are not well disciplined in the Way of Buddha. How can they ever expect to be the leaders of all beings?

Plate 5. Rinzai at Work

A true man of non-doing,
Surely in indignation!

Sengai has substituted Zen
master Rinzai's favorite saying "the true man of no-
title" by Lao-tzu's term
"non-doing" (wu-wei). As
"non-doing" is too often
mistaken for doing no
work, or indolence, or pas-
sivity, Sengai demonstrates
here how hard Zen masters
must work, even to the
point of indignation, to
help their fellow beings
open their eyes to the presence of "the true man of
no-title" in each.

Plate 6. Kyogen Sweeping the Ground

One strike made him forget
his learning.
What kind of sound was it?
A piece of brick immediately
Turned itself into gold.

Zen monk Kyogen (Hsiang-yen) of China was a disciple of Isan (Wei-shan, 771-853). He was fond of keeping notes of his masters, and thought a great deal of them. One day, he found out that all the notes and knowledge he had accumulated were after all of no use in really understanding Zen. He then burned them, and being so disappointed at his inability to gain satori, he decided not to go on with this pursuit. He retired to a country temple where he devoted himself to looking after an old master's graveyard. One day, while sweeping the ground, it happened that a piece of stone swept away by his broom struck a bamboo nearby. The sound thus produced awakened his mind to a state of enlightenment. He composed a poem in which this "one strike" is referred to.

Sengai now asks: "What kind of sound was it that made Kyogen come to a realization?" He answers in the last two lines.

Plate 7. The Autumn Moon

To see or not to see—
That's man's business:
[Yet,] the autumn moon!

Whether you see or do not see me, that is a human affair. As for me, the autumn moon, I radiate my beams on the world impartially and uniformly.

Below the moon, Sengai depicts human beings in their various postures—the blind man with the musical instrument serenading, another looking above, while the other two are indulging in their respective pleasures. The truth is ever there, as bright and impartial as the autumn moon shining upon blind and seer alike. But each of us will enjoy himself in accordance with his caliber, temperament and karma.

Plate 8. Shoki the Devil-driver

The May showers are here.
Let us pray to Shoki
To clear away all evil influences.

Shoki (Chung-kuei) is a legendary Chinese figure that destroys evil creatures. He is generally represented as wearing a dark colored robe, and a crushed cap, and has a fearsome look with a thickly growing beard. He carries a sword to drive away the devils.

Once he appeared to a Chinese Emperor of the T'ang suffering from a high fever. The Emperor dreamt that Shoki was chasing a smallish devil whom he had caught stealing a jade flute and a perfume bag from the imperial bedroom and was then eating him up. The Emperor asked his name, and he replied, "My name is Shoki and I am requiting a favor I once received from you." When the Emperor awoke from his dream, he found the fever had altogether left him.

The fifth day of the fifth month is Boy's Day, five being the symbol for the male principle. This is the time to wish protection for every male child from harm of every sort. Shoki is called upon to play his part.

mind. But perhaps you feel that to remain in it is too tough a job? If so, listen and try to grasp the meaning of what I say. Stop piling up evil deeds, stop being a demon, a hungry ghost, an animal. Keep your distance from those things that transform you in that way, and you'll attain the Buddha-mind once and for all. Don't you see?

LAYMAN: I do, and I am convinced.

6.

PRIEST: When you are successful in making me think of my birthlessness, I find myself feeling idle all day.

BANKEI: One in the Buddha-mind is far from idle. When you are not in it, when you sell it, so to speak, for worthless things you happen to be attached to, then you are being idle.

The priest remained silent.

BANKEI: Remain in non-birth, and you will never be idle.

7.

PRIEST: Once in the Buddha-mind, I am absent-minded.

BANKEI: Well, suppose you are absent-minded as you say. If someone pricked you in the back with a gimlet, would you feel the pain?

PRIEST: Naturally!

BANKEI: Then you are not absent-minded. Feeling the pain, your mind would show itself to be alert. Follow my exhortation: remain in the Buddha-mind.

8.

PRIEST: I often find myself straying from the Buddha-mind. Perhaps it's that I haven't yet seen the truth. Please help me.

BANKEI: The parent-begotten birthless mind is possessed by all, and none truly strays from it if he is aware of doing so. It is that you turn the Buddha-mind into something else. I repeat: aware of the Buddha-mind, you cannot have strayed. Understand? Even in the deepest sleep you're not away from it.

Whether here or at home, remain just as you are now, listening to my exhortation, and you'll feel firmly in the Buddha-mind. It's only when you're greedy or selfish that you feel yourself astray. Remember this: there isn't a sinful person who was born that way. Take the case of the thief. He wasn't born that way. Perhaps when a child he happened to have a sinful idea, acted upon it, and let the habit develop of itself. When apprehended and questioned he will of course speak of an inborn tendency. Nonsense! Show him he's wrong, and he will give up stealing, and in so doing he can immediately attain the everlasting Buddha-mind.

In my home town there lived a pickpocket who was so skillful he could tell at a glance how much money was being carried by someone approaching. When finally nabbed and imprisoned for a few years, he started to change his ways, and when set free he became a sculptor of Buddhist images. He died a holy death, praying to Amitabha for eternal salvation. This shows what a man who repents past conduct is capable of. I tell you no one is born to sin. It's all a question of will.

9.

LAYMAN: Though I undertake Zen discipline, I often find myself lazy, weary of the whole thing, unable to advance.

BANKEI: Once in the Buddha-mind there's no need to advance, nor is it possible to recede. Once in birthlessness, to attempt to advance is to recede from the state of non-birth. A man secure in this state need not bother himself with such things: he's above them.

10.

LAYMAN: They say you're able to read minds. Is that true?

BANKEI: No such thing happens in our sect. Even if one of us should possess supernatural powers, being in the birthless Buddha-mind he would not use it. I suppose you think I have such powers because I'm always commenting on your personal affairs, but really I'm no different from you. In the Buddha-mind all have the same gifts, for all puzzles are solved by it, all problems overcome. Non-birth is really a very practical doctrine. By criticizing, the master hopes to instruct: that's the long and short of it. And that's why I'm always being so personal. Oh, we're very down-to-earth here!

11.

PRIEST: For a long time now I've been trying to understand the story of Hyakujo and the Fox (The second koan in *Mumonkan,* which concerns a monk who had been transformed into a fox because of his denial of cause-and-effect, and who was enlightened by the master Hyakujo's affirmation of it.), but it's beyond me—probably because I haven't involved myself in wholehearted contemplation. Please enlighten me.

BANKEI: We shouldn't concern ourselves with such old wives' tales. The trouble is you're still ignorant of the Buddha-mind which, birthless and immaculate, unties any and every knot.

12.

PRIEST (on hearing Bankei chasten the priest of the foregoing): Do you mean to say all the old Zen-men's words and questions are useless?

BANKEI: The old masters' answers were given on the spot to questions asked them, but those questions and their given answers should not concern us. Of course, I'm in no position to say what use they have, but one thing I know: once in the Buddha-mind, one need not fret over them. All your attention is given to irrelevant matters; you stray. Most dangerous!

13.

The Buddha-mind in each of you is immaculate. All you've done is reflected in it, but if you bother about one such reflection, you're certain to stray. Your thoughts don't lie deep enough—they rise from the shallows of your mind.

Remember that all you see and hear is reflected in the Buddha-mind and influenced by what was previously seen and heard. Needless to say, thoughts aren't entities. So if you permit them to rise, reflect themselves, or cease altogether as they're prone to do, and if you don't worry about them, you'll never stray. In this way let one hundred, nay, one thousand thoughts arise, and it's as if not one has arisen. You will remain undisturbed.

14.

PRIESTESSES OF THE VINAYA SCHOOL [a sect of Buddhism that emphasizes formal monastic rules]: Can we enter nirvana by simply observing the priestess' two hundred and fifty commandments?

BANKEI: One who doesn't drink wine need not be told he shouldn't. Questions of omission or commission apply only to bad priests and priestesses. If the Vinaya sect makes a merit of obeying commandments, it's merely admitting the presence of sinful members. Stay in the Buddha-mind of non-birth, and such considerations will prove unnecessary.

15.

BANKEI: The bell rings, but you hear the sound before it rings. The mind that is aware of the bell before it rings is the Buddha-mind. If however you hear the bell and then say it is a bell, you are merely naming what's been born, a thing of minor importance.

16.

The only thing I tell my people is to stay in the Buddha-mind. There are no regulations, no formal discipline. Nevertheless they have agreed among themselves to sit in Zen for a period of two incense sticks [an hour or so] daily. All right, let them. But they should understand that the birthless Buddha-mind has absolutely nothing to do with sitting with an incense stick burning in front of you. If one keeps in the Buddha-mind without straying, there's no further satori to seek. Whether asleep or awake, one is a living Buddha. Zazen means only one thing—sitting tranquilly in the Buddha-mind. But really, you know, one's everyday life, in its entirety, should be thought of as a kind of sitting in Zen.

Even during one's formal sitting, one may leave one's seat to attend to something. In my temple, at least, such things are allowed. Indeed it's sometimes advisable to walk in Zen for one incense stick's burning, and sit in Zen for the other. A natural thing, after all. One can't sleep all day, so one rises. One can't talk all day, so one engages in zazen. There are no binding rules here.

Most masters these days use devices (koan, etc.) to teach, and they seem to value these devices above all else—they can't get to the truth directly. They're little more than blind fools! Another bit of their stupidity is to hold that, according to Zen, unless one has a doubt he proceeds to smash, he's good for nothing. Of course, all this forces people to have doubts. No, they never teach the importance of staying in the birthless Buddha-mind. They would make of it a lump of doubt. A very serious mistake.

Prayers and Sermons

XII. TANZAN (1819–1892, Soto)

Though Tanzan had his satori certified by Fugai, he became successor to Kyosan, the master who had converted him from Confucianism to Buddhism. Tanzan was a scholar as well as a born Zennist: he was the first holder of the Chair of Indian Philosophy at Tokyo University and, later, president of the Soto Sect College in Tokyo. He was also interested in European science, especially physiology and medicine, and was an essay writer of distinction on a variety of subjects, the most memorable probably being those on what he called "the identity of ignorance and sickness" and related themes. Through the study of the sutras, and his own experiments, he reached the conclusion that the real cause of sickness is to be found in ignorance, that is, illusion, in the Buddhist sense. By means of his Zen power, he carried out experiments on himself which, he admitted, made him dangerously ill three times. Briefly, he felt ignorance to be a form of mental disturbance, agony a form of delusion the ordinary person suffers. Thus Tanzan's theory has much in common with psychosomatic medicine. Of course, the remedy he offered was Zen, that is No-mind. A man in No-mind can remain in health. Tanzan was totally convinced of the verity of his discovery, that is, what causes ignorance is the spinal fluid which flows up into the brain, then circulates it, the ignorance, throughout the body. After a life rich in experience, and about which there are numerous anecdotes, he died on the day he had predicted.

The observations below are from *Tanzan-osho Zenshu* (Master Tanzan's Complete Works, 1909). We do not present any of the essays on the identity of ignorance and sickness and the influence of spinal fluid, because of their problematic quality.

89

How to Grasp Buddha's Teaching and the Mind

1. An ancient justly said, "One can't grasp Buddha's teaching without a seeing eye." Yet most people have no such eye and, adhering to words and phrases, end up by being mere annotators. In order to appraise writings, one must be able to judge properly. Hence the saying, "Let a man of proper understanding teach an erroneous doctrine, and it becomes a right doctrine. Let a man of erroneous understanding teach a right doctrine, and it becomes a false doctrine." A man of discernment makes no mistake in his appraisal, he does not take white for black.

An old master once said, "All the seven hundred disciples of Gunin [the Fifth Patriarch of China] 'understood' Buddhism. It was his new disciple Eno alone who did not. Therefore Eno succeeded his master as the Sixth Patriarch." It should be known by all that discrimination is to the mind what oil is to wheat flour: dualism is a chain. Ancients underwent twenty or thirty years of serious training, as if in mourning for their parents or doctoring their sick hearts. Then, and then alone, could they attain perfect awakening, impossible to those whose knowledge is inferior to that of mere sutra commentators and who cling to stupid discriminations.

I have been reading various commentaries on the sutras, etc., and have found that though the writers show themselves to possess rather deep knowledge, not one has escaped the curse of dualism. This has convinced me anew that Yakusan (751–834), the Chinese master, was right when he prohibited sutra reading to his followers. My advice to those whose eyes have not yet been opened to the truth—leap from the net and see how immense is the ocean.

2. The law of the mind is above human understanding, for the mind is timeless and permeates all. Its function is not merely that of perception and cognition. It is limitless, containing all phenomena—mountains, rivers, the whole universe. A fan can soar skyward, a toad fly, yet never outside the mind.

In other religions and philosophies the so-called mind is looked upon as the governor of the body or the lord of things. Which is the outcome of speculation, or stupid reason. Once let the self arise, and it is bound to be shackled by myriad things. The sentient body is composed of four elements—earth, water, fire, wind—while insentient things naturally exist each in its proper state. What, then, is governor, lord? Neither the body nor things have a ruler, the whole concept of rulership being a product of the fettered dichotomous mind. Solely because they have not understood the mind, it would seem, the followers of non-Buddhist teachings have always gone astray.

XIII. Harada-Sogaku (1871–1961, Soto)

Mumonkan, a collection of forty-eight koans compiled and commented upon by the Chinese master Mumon Ekai (1183–1260) is along with *Hekiganroku* (used mainly by the Rinzai sect) and *Shoyoroku* (used by the Soto sect), one of the chief koan compilations. Among modern commentaries on the work, the outstanding are those by Nantembo, Sugawara-Jiho, Iida-Toin, Inoue-Shuten, and Jimpo-Nyoten. More recent commentaries of value are those by Yamamoto-Gempo, Asahina-Sogen, and that of our author, Harada-Sogaku, which has been chosen as a specimen of modern Zen commentary, in spite of the fact that Harada-Sogaku was an eminent Soto master, not a Rinzai—though he did undergo for a time Rinzai training. The author of around forty books, he had throughout his long life many serious aspirants after Buddhahood among his disciples, more than ten of whom were foreigners.

On *"Gutei Lifts His Finger,"* Third Koan of Mumonkan

1. Text of the koan:

Master Gutei simply lifted his finger when questioned about Zen. One day a visitor asked the boy attending Gutei to give the substance of his master's teaching, at which the boy lifted his finger.

Learning of what had happened, Gutei summoned the boy and without a word of warning cut off his finger. The boy ran off, howling. Gutei called after him, and when the boy stopped to look back, the master raised his finger. At that instant the boy gained satori.

When about to die, Gutei gathered his followers

about him and said, "I gained my one-finger Zen from Master Tenryu, and a lifetime couldn't deplete it."

With this the master breathed his last.

2. Mumon's comment:

The satori attained by Gutei and the boy had nothing to do with the finger. If you can see into their awakening, you will be at one with Tenryu, Gutei, and the boy.

Note: Very little is known of the lives of Gutei and Tenryu. The latter was a disciple of Daibai, whose own master was the famous Baso (—788).

3. Mumon's summary in verse:

> Gutei ridiculed old Tenryu
> And sharply tried the boy.
> The god used but a single hand
> To rip open Mount Kazan.

4. Harada-Sogaku's lecture on the text:

In spite of considering himself a mediocrity and having little hope of gaining satori, Master Gutei pursued Zen seriously. An awakening was his deepest desire, and he must have felt that with the help of a Bodhisattva he would experience one, if not in this life then in the next. It was, he felt, the Bodhisattva Gutei-Kwannon who could help him, and he recited the *dharani* (incantation) dedicated to him constantly. "Gutei," the name given him, comes from the *dharani*.

The story goes that one day the nun Jissai came to see Gutei. Hatted and shod as a voyager, she paced around him three times, then, thumping the floor with her staff, said, "If you say the word, I'll remove my hat." She repeated this three times, but Gutei did not answer. She was about to leave in utter contempt of him when he said, "It's getting dark. Why not stay?"

"If you say the word," she said, "I'll stay."

Again Gutei was tongue-tied, and Jissai walked off.

Gutei was humiliated by all this, of course, especially as it had been a nun who had made a fool of him. Then and there he made up his mind to go the following morning to a well-known master for training, and he packed his things. While he was dozing the guardian god appeared before him and said, "It's all very well that you've decided on training, but don't leave your temple. In a few days a flesh-and-blood Bodhisattva will come to teach you."

The dream came true, for a few days later Master Tenryu, a disciple of Daibai, arrived. Gutei, full of gratitude, told him what had happened and concluded by asking, "Will you be good enough to turn for me the Wheel of the exquisite Dharma?" At this the master thrust a finger at Gutei's nose, and Gutei had a perfect satori. Now he was a genuine Zen priest, and remained in his temple.

There is another famous story connected with a nun, though it has nothing to do with Gutei. It seems that a group of seventeen monks from the province of Shoku in China, all of them in search of Zen enlightenment, traveled to Mount Gyozan. There they sought out the celebrated Master Ejaku, who lived on the mountain, for guidance. It was arranged that they stay the night in a small temple attached to the large one. That evening they discussed one of the koans related to the Sixth Patriarch of China: "What moves is not the wind nor the banner, but your mind."

Now, the nun Myoshinni, who presided over the temple, happened to hear their conversation and made a scathing criticism of it to her followers. "Humbug!" she said. "They're all blind fools in there." One of the nuns attending the monks told them of her teacher's opinion. If they had not been true Zen followers they might have dismissed Myoshinni's comment as a piece of impertinence, but they were ardent in their quest of enlightenment and they humbly begged her instruction.

On entering the nun's room together, they were asked to approach closer. While they were doing so, the nun said, "What moves is not the wind, nor the banner, nor your mind." At once all seventeen monks awakened. Which shows how much they desired Zen and what perfectly clean slates were their minds.

You must not think this story a mere wives' tale. You also, if your minds are clean slates, can attain satori. The monks of the story, I should add, did not remain to climb Mount Gyozan to see the master, but returned home, anxious to teach.

There were some other remarkable women Zennists in China. One was Ryutetsuma, another was the old woman who burned down the hermitage, and still another the woman of the teahouse near Godaizan. In Japan, and more recently, there was Old Osatsu, the disciple of Hakuin. In Buddhism, as in most things, more men than women achieve distinction, but women do seem to excel in mind-control and single-heartedness.

But I've digressed. Gutei was not a learned man, and thus had to resort to one-finger Zen. But there have been a number of masters who would make unvaried answers to Zen questions. Thinking of China, there was, for instance, Tachi, who would strike the ground with his staff. To see what would happen if the master did not have his staff, a monk once hid it and asked him, "What is the fundamental meaning of Buddhism?" At which Tachi shouted a *kwatz* [Zen cry]. To any question asked him, Shakkyo drew his bow taut, as if about to send an arrow through the questioner's heart. Mugo's answer, on the other hand, was invariably, "Rid yourself of illusion," and Shiko's, "Look at the dog." Tokusan was perhaps the most original: he would strike his questioner with his staff.

It is not easy to grasp Gutei's one-finger Zen. However, once doing so, you will have finished your Zen training. All that is required is identification with the finger and the forgetting of self. Annihilate all with it —wind, rain, eating, urinating. What is it, after all? Be that finger, and you've won the universe!

"One day a visitor asked the boy attending Gutei to give the substance of his master's teaching, at which the boy lifted his finger."* The boy learned to imitate Gutei's trick. When in Gutei's absence a monk came and asked about the master's doctrine, the boy raised his finger. When Gutei learned of this, he knew that the time was ripe for the boy. You all know what followed.

Now, how does this compare with Hakuin's "Sound of One Hand Clapping" or Joshu's "Nothingness"? The *Mumonkan* contains forty-eight koans, and each is a perfect exposition of Buddhism. Whatever koan I happen to be lecturing on, if you are studying the koan of Mu, relate all that I say to it; if you are studying "One Hand," relate all that I say to it. And so on. The same

* From the "Text of the koan," p. 92.

holds true for breath-counting exercises or the sitting-only method. These, as you know, are but devices to get you to open your eyes, and if you succeed in solving one koan, you will be able to handle them all. Don't give up halfway. Remember, the later the satori, the better the results, for it's very likely that you will have penetrated it completely.

5. Lecture on comment:

Some may think that Gutei's satori and the boy's too had much to do with the perishable finger. Well, they're on the wrong track. Satori can't be found in a finger; rather it's the "original face" thrust under your very nose. It is exactly that which utters "Mu." It is "Mu" itself, as well as the "Sound of One Hand Clapping." If you are ready for it, it is yours. If not, you can climb the highest mountain for it—in vain. It is always there: the willow is green, the peony scarlet; the mountain is high, the sea full. No, you can't cut the "One Finger" with a knife.

Once the mystery of the finger is cleared up, you will not only understand Gutei and the boy, but be the friend of Buddha and Amitabha. You will see through everyone. No longer will life and death be problems. That is what is meant by "You will be at one with Tenryu, Gutei, and the boy."

6. Lecture on summary:

An ancient myth of China goes that the god split Mount Kain, calling one half Kainzan, the other Shuyo-zan, and thus making possible a flow of water, put an end to a great flood. Now, you may admire the compe-tent Gutei who ripped the boy's finger as if it were a mountain of illusion, but really, you know, Gutei is little more than a laughingstock. Was he not taken in by old Tenryu? And the lifting of that finger—what did it amount to, after all?

My admonition, then: Be a great fool! You know, don't you, that there was a master who called himself just that? Now, a petty fool is nothing but a worldling, but a Great Fool is a Buddha. (The word "ridiculed" is very important here.) Sakyamuni and Amitabha are themselves Great Fools, are they not? Oh, we're all smart fellows here—therefore, good for nothing. Smartness, after all, is worldly wisdom, one of the eight hindrances to the attainment of Buddhahood. Once Great Saigo [1827–1877, a leading figure in the Meiji era] said of the layman Yamaoka-Tesshu, "I'm no match for one who cares nothing for money, fame, or even life itself." A Great Fool is in reality a man of great wisdom, seen in this light. Tesshu's life is a case in point.

So much for the first line of the gatha. The second glorifies the Great Fool's accomplishments. When the boy lifted his finger in reply to Gutei's question, off went the finger. Oh, his wisdom, his skill, his *mercy!*

Seccho praises Gutei highly in the *Hekiganroku*. I have reference to the nineteenth koan: "Where in the world is another like him?" In the last two lines of the poem, Mumon extols Gutei's finger, which proved itself as effective as the hand of a god.

All of you gathered here before me should not pass lightly over the one-finger koan. It is far, far more than an old tale. Put heart and soul into its penetration— achieve Buddhahood!

ANECDOTES

When Ninagawa-Shinzaemon, linked-verse poet and Zen devotee, heard that Ikkyu (1394–1481, Rinzai), abbot of the famous Daitokuji in Murasakino (violet field) of Kyoto, was a remarkable master, he desired to become his disciple. He called on Ikkyu and the following dialogue took place at the temple entrance:

IKKYU: Who are you?
NINAGAWA: A devotee of Buddhism.
IKKYU: You are from?
NINAGAWA: Your region.
IKKYU: Ah. And what's happening there these days?
NINAGAWA: The crows caw, the sparrows twitter.
IKKYU: And where do you think you are now?
NINAGAWA: In a field dyed violet.
IKKYU: Why?
NINAGAWA: Miscanthus, morning glories, safflowers, chrysanthemums, asters.
IKKYU: And after they're gone?
NINAGAWA: It's Miyagino (field known for its autumn flowering).
IKKYU: What happens in the field?
NINAGAWA: The stream flows through, the wind sweeps over.

Amazed at Ninagawa's Zen-like speech, Ikkyu led him to his room and served him tea. Then he spoke the following impromptu verse:

> I want to serve
> You delicacies.
> Alas! the Zen sect
> Can offer nothing.

At which the visitor replied:

> The mind which treats me
> To nothing is the original void—
> A delicacy of delicacies.

Deeply moved, the master said, "My son, you have learned much."

2

One day the Lord Mihara ordered a painter to do a picture for him, and a few weeks later the artist brought him a picture of a wild goose. As soon as his eyes fell on the painting, the lord cried out, "Wild geese fly side by side. Your picture is symbolic of revolt!"

The lord's attendants, frightened out of their wits, sought out Motsugai (1792–1867, Soto), a formidable Zen master, who, besides being a favorite of the lord, was a man of great strength and talent. He was nicknamed Fist Bonze because he could punch a hole in a board, and he was also a good lancer and an expert horseman. But more important to the lord's attendants, he was very wise and skilled with the pen.

Motsugai hastened to Lord Mihara and, casting but a glance at the picture, wrote the following over the painted bird:

> The first wild goose!
> Another and another and another
> In endless succession.

Lord Mihara's good humor was restored, and both the artist and Motsugai were generously rewarded.

3

Kato-Dewanokami-Yasuoki, lord of Osu in the province of Iyo, was passionate about the military arts. One day the great master Bankei called on him and, as they sat face to face, the young lord grasped his spear and made as if to pierce Bankei. But the master silently flicked its head aside with his rosary and said, "No good. You're too worked up."

Years later Yasuoki, who had become a great spearsman, spoke of Bankei as the one who had taught him most about the art.

4

Date-Jitoku, a fine waka poet and a retainer of Lord Tokugawa, wanted to master Zen, and with this in mind made an appointment to see Ekkei, abbot of Shokokuji in Kyoto and one widely known for his rigorous training methods. Jitoku was ambitious and went to the master full of hopes for the interview. As soon as he entered Ekkei's room, however, even before being able to utter a word, he received a blow.

He was, of course, astonished, but as it is a strict rule of Zen to do or say nothing unless asked by the master, he withdrew silently. He had never been so mortified. No one had ever dared strike him before, not even his lord. He went at once to Dokuon, who was to succeed Ekkei as abbot, and told him that he planned to challenge the rude and daring master to a duel.

"Can't you see that the master was being kind to you?" said Dokuon. "Exert yourself in zazen, and you'll discover for yourself what his treatment of you means."

For three days and nights Jitoku engaged in desperate contemplation, then, suddenly, he experienced an ecstatic awakening. This, his satori, was approved by Ekkei.

Jitoku called on Dokuon again and after thanking him for the advice said, "If it hadn't been for your wisdom, I would never have had so transfiguring an experience. As for the master, well, his blow was far from hard enough."

5

Kanzan (1277–1360, Rinzai), the National Teacher, gave Fujiwara-Fujifusa the koan "Original Perfection." For many days Fujifusa sat in Zen. When he finally had an intuition, he composed the following:

Once possessed of the mind that has always been,
Forever I'll benefit men and devas both.
The benignity of the Buddha and Patriarchs can hardly
    be repaid.
Why should I be reborn as horse or donkey?

When he called on Kanzan with the poem, this dialogue took place:

KANZAN: Where's the mind?
FUJIFUSA: It fills the great void.
KANZAN: With what will you benefit men and devas?
FUJIFUSA: I shall saunter along the stream, or sit down to watch the gathering clouds.
KANZAN: Just how do you intend repaying the Buddha and Patriarchs?
FUJIFUSA: The sky's over my head, the earth under my feet.
KANZAN: All right, but why shouldn't you be reborn as horse or donkey?

At this Fujifusa got to his feet and bowed.
"Good!" Kanzan said with a loud laugh. "You've gained perfect satori."

6

Ken-O and his disciple Menzan (1683–1769, Soto) were eating a melon together. Suddenly the master asked, "Tell me, where does all this sweetness come from?"

"Why," Menzan quickly swallowed and answered, "it's a product of cause and effect."

"Bah! That's cold logic!"

"Well," Menzan said, "from where then?"

"From that very 'where' itself, that's where."

7

There was to be a big party at the house of the Chief
Minister of the Kuroda Clan of Hakata, and both
Kamei-Shoyo, the famous Confucian scholar, and the
master Sengai (1750–1837, Rinzai) were invited. The
host informed Sengai that the great teacher would be
present, implying that the master, who was indifferent
to worldly matters, would have to come dressed for the
occasion.

On the appointed day Sengai entered the mansion
wearing a costume of white, violet, and gold. His rosary
was of amethyst and he even carried a ceremony-fan.
Followed by his disciples, he crossed the room in great
dignity.

Of course, the sight of Sengai's getup was hateful to
Shoyo, and he couldn't restrain himself from calling
out, "Master, why did you come dressed as a fine lady?"

At this the other guests held their breath.

Sengai smiled and, moving straight up to Shoyo,
whacked him on the head with his fan, and said, "Why,
it was to give birth to this fine gentleman."

8

A wealthy man invited Sengai to a housewarming and, after serving him a fine meal, asked him to write a poem in honor of the occasion. Sengai quickly wrote down the first half of a waka, which made the host, who had been hovering over his shoulder, extremely angry. It read:

> The house is surrounded
> By the gods of poverty.

Ignoring the host and the guests, who on being informed of what he had written looked daggers at him, Sengai smoked his pipe in silence. Suddenly he grasped his brush and completed the poem with these lines:

> How can the deities of good luck
> Ever leave it?

When the host and the guests read these lines there was great rejoicing, and all praised Sengai warmly.

9

Murata-Shuko, one of the most eminent tea masters of his day, visited Ikkyu and was asked what he thought of Master Joshu's well-known reference to tea drinking. Shuko made no reply and, at last, Ikkyu served him a cup of tea.

As Shuko lifted the cup to his lips, Ikkyu suddenly let out with a *kwatz* and smashed the cup with his iron *nyoi* (Buddhist implement).

Shuko made a deep bow.

"What are you like," Ikkyu asked, "when you've no intention of taking tea?"

Without answering, Shuko got up and moved toward the door.

"Stop," Ikkyu called. "What are you like when you've taken tea?"

"The willow is green," Shuko said, "the rose is red."

Ikkyu, approving Shuko's grasp of Zen, smiled broadly.

10

Settan (1801–1873, Rinzai) and Sozan (1798–1867, Rinzai), the greatest masters of their day, came to an important ceremony at the Myoshin Temple. Settan belonged to the Inzan branch of their sect, Sozan to the Takuju branch, and as had been expected by all present they at once began a Zen engagement in a room of the temple to which no one else was allowed entry.

So horrible to the ears was the dispute, the whole temple was frightened. They shouted kwatz and their staffs clashed like swords.

All at once from out of nowhere appeared a middle-aged priest who, head wrapped in a towel, a saké bottle bobbing from his sash, robe tucked between the legs, began to sing at the top of his voice a popular song:

Looking down from the top of the mountain, O!
The valley's a bed of melons and eggplants, O!
    Arya, don, don, don!
    Korya, don, don, don!

Dancing crazily, he barged into the prohibited room.

At the sight of him the astonished Sozan turned to his rival and demanded, "Whose disciple is this?"

"Mine!" Settan said triumphantly. "That's my Keichu." (1824–1905, Rinzai)

"You're lucky in your disciples," Sozan said. "I'm beaten."

Both masters laughed long together, and Settan, who had trained Keichu for more than ten years, saw that he had finally grasped the truth of Zen.

11

The master Fugai (1779–1847, Soto), a fine painter and a successor to Motsugai, the famous Fist Bonze, was considered very wise and generous, yet he was most severe, both to himself and his disciples. He went to a mountain cave to sit in Zen, and when hungry would come to the village for scraps.

One day a monk called Bundo, attracted by Fugai's austerities, called at the cave and asked the master whether he could spend the night. The master seemed happy to put him up, and next morning prepared rice gruel for him, but not having an extra bowl, he went out and returned with a skull found lying near a tomb. He filled it with gruel and offered it to Bundo. The guest refused to touch it, and stared at Fugai as if he thought him mad. At this Fugai became furious and drove him from the cave with blows. "Fool!" he shouted after him, "how can you, with your worldly notions of filth and purity, think yourself a Buddhist?"

Some months later the master Tetsugyu visited him and told him frankly that he thought it a great pity that he had so completely forsaken the world.

Fugai laughed loudly and said, "Oh, it's easy enough to forsake the world and become a bonze. The difficult thing is then to become a true Buddhist."

It is told that Fugai met his end in an extraordinary manner. Feeling his last day had come, he quickly had a hole dug and, standing in it with great dignity, had himself covered with earth.

12

Sato-Kaiseki was very much disturbed by the implications of Copernicus' heliocentric theory, which, of course, was inconsistent with the old Buddhist cosmology in which Mount Sumeru occupies the center of the universe. He reasoned that if the Buddhist view of the cosmos were proved false, the triple world and the twenty-five forms of existence would be reduced to nonsense, resulting in the negation of Buddhism itself. Immediately he set about writing a book in defense of the Mount Sumeru position, sparing himself no effort as a champion of Buddhism.

When he had finished the work, he took it at once to Master Ekido and presented it to him triumphantly. After leafing through only the first few pages, however, the master thrust the book back and, shaking his head, said, "How stupid! Don't you realize that the basic aim of Buddhism is to shatter the triple world and the twenty-five forms of existence? Why stick to such utterly worthless things and treasure Mount Sumeru? Blockhead!"

Dumfounded, Kaiseki shoved the book under his arm and went quickly home.

13

Gasan (1853–1900, Rinzai), a distinguished master of the important Tenryuji Temple of Kyoto, was very fond of saké, which made him like many other Zen priests. He would say: "One *go* of saké and I'm vivacious, five *go* and I'm mild as a spring day, one *sho* (ten *go*) and the wintry moon is high in the sky, the carp leaps from the deep pond."

Once after being treated to drink in downtown Kyoto he returned to the temple in the evening almost helplessly drunk. As it was time for *dokusan*, the monks were overjoyed, for they expected the master, who always made dokusan a bitter trial for them, to be lenient for once.

When one by one they entered Gasan's room, however, they found him sitting more solemn than ever, eyes glaring at the doorway.

14

Muso (1275–1351, Rinzai), the National Teacher and one of the most illustrious masters of his day, left the capital in the company of a disciple for a distant province. On reaching the Tenryu river they had to wait for an hour before boarding the ferry; just as it was about to leave the shore, a drunken samurai ran up and leapt into the packed boat, nearly swamping it. He tottered wildly as the small craft made its way across the river and, fearing for the safety of the passengers, the ferryman begged him to stand quietly.

"We're like sardines in here!" the samurai said gruffly. Then, pointing to Muso, "Why not toss out the bonze?"

"Please be patient," Muso said. "We'll reach the other side soon."

"What!" bawled the samurai. "Me be patient? Listen here, if you don't jump off this thing and start swimming, I swear I'll drown you!"

The master's continued calm so infuriated the samurai that he struck Muso's head with his iron fan, drawing blood. Muso's disciple had had enough by this time and, as he was a powerful man, wanted to challenge the samurai on the spot. "I can't permit him to go on living after this," he said to the master.

"Why get so worked up over a trifle?" Muso said with a smile. "It's exactly in matters of this kind that the bonze's training proves itself. Patience, you must remember, is more than just a word." He then recited an extempore waka:

> The beater and the beaten:
> Mere players of a game
> Ephemeral as a dream.

When the boat reached shore and Muso and his disciple got off, the samurai ran up and prostrated himself at the master's feet. Then and there he became a disciple of the master.

15

One winter day a masterless samurai came to Eizai's (1141–1215, Rinzai) temple and made an appeal. "I'm poor and sick," he said, "and my family's dying of hunger. Please help us, master."

Eizai, whose life, dependent as he was on widows' mites, was extremely austere, had nothing whatsoever to give the man. He was about to send him off when he remembered the image of Yakushi-Buddha in the hall. Going up to it, he tore off its halo and gave it to the samurai. "Sell this," he said, "it should tide you over."

The bewildered but desperate samurai took the halo and left.

"But, master," cried one of Eizai's disciples, "it's a sacrilege! How could you have been so reckless?"

"Reckless? Bah! Have you never heard how the Chinese master Tanka (–834) burned a wooden image of the Buddha to warm himself? Surely what I've done isn't half as bad, is it? I've merely put the Buddha's mind, which is full of love and mercy, to use, so to speak. Indeed if he himself had heard that poor samurai, he'd have cut off a limb for him!"

16

Hakuju (1836–   , Obaku), who had played the principal role in resuscitating, in the Meiji era, the Obaku sect, served as a distinguished lecturer at the Tendai Sect College. One hot summer afternoon as he lectured with customary zeal on the Chinese classics he noticed that a few of the students were dozing off. He stopped lecturing in midsentence and said, "It is hot, isn't it? Can't blame you for going to sleep. Mind if I join you?"

With this, Hakuju shut his textbook, and leaning well back in his chair fell asleep. The class was dumfounded, and those who had been dozing were wakened by his snores. All sat straight up in their seats and waited for the master to awaken.

17

After six months of instructing the Regent Hojo-Tokiyori in Zen, Dogen left Kamakura for his temple in Echizen, having declined to take over the temple the grateful Tokiyori had built for him. Thus he lived up to his motto that priests should have little or nothing to do with the powerful.

Soon after, one of his followers who had remained behind on business returned with a title to three thousand *kan* of land in Echizen, the gift of Tokiyori. Jubilantly he showed the title around to his fellow monks, then, full of expectation, presented it with a low bow to Dogen.

The master glanced at the title and handed it back with a scowl. "How sordid!" he said. "You know I don't preach for gain of any kind. Else why shouldn't I have accepted that fine temple in Kamakura? Those like yourself who curry favor with the great befoul the path of Buddhas and patriarchs. Your sort stains all you touch—leave this temple at once."

The monk remained speechless before Dogen, who suddenly rose and, snatching off the monk's robe, drove him away. And that wasn't all: the master had the part of the floor where the monk had sat in Zen cut away and the earth below it dug to a depth of six feet.

18

During three years of severe training under the great master Gizan, Koshu (1839–1905, Rinzai) was unable to gain satori. At the beginning of a special seven-day session of discipline, he thought his chance had finally come. He climbed the tower of the temple gate and, going up to the Arhat images, made this vow: "Either I realize my dreams up here, or they'll find my dead body at the foot of the tower!"

He went without food or sleep, giving himself up to constant zazen, often crying out in his torment things like, "What was my karma that in spite of all these efforts I can't grasp the Way?"

At last Koshu admitted his failure and, determined to make an end of it, advanced to the railing and slowly lifted a leg over it. At that very instant he had an awakening. Overjoyed, he rushed down the stairs and through the rain to Gizan's room.

"Bravo!" cried the master before Koshu had a chance to speak. "You've finally had your day!"

19

Tanzan (1819–1892, Soto), a rare master, once officiated as *indoshi* (leader) at a funeral. Facing the coffin, he formally made a great circle in the air with a firebrand. And now all the attendants awaited the customary splendid phrases. But the master's mouth was clamped shut.

Then while the attendants stared in amazement the rays of the setting sun fell directly on the master's bald head, seeming to scorch it. "Hot!" Tanzan said. "Hot! Oh hot!" He then made a slight bow to the coffin and returned to his place.

Needless to say, the attendants remained puzzled long after the coffin had been settled in the earth.

20

Ex-Emperor: Gudo, what happens to the man of enlightenment and the man of illusion after death?

Gudo: How should I know, sir?

Ex-Emperor: Why, because you're a master!

Gudo: Yes, sir, but no dead one!

21

Oishi-Yoshio (1657–1703), leader of the famous forty-seven Ronin, was a disciple of Bankei. When he had finally succeeded in penetrating the master's "Birthlessness," he went to him to present his view. Approving, the master pointed to an inkstone and said, "This is Saigyo's [1118–1190] workmanship."

"Why no," Oishi replied. "I myself made it before Saigyo was born!"

"What you produced is rightfully yours," Bankei said and gave the inkstone to the loyal retainer.

22

Dokuon (1819–1895, Rinzai) was very sick, and Tekisui (1822–1899, Rinzai) came to ask after him. Entering the sickroom, he announced himself, then straddled Dokuon. With his face almost touching Dokuon's, he said, "Well, how are you?"

"Sick," answered Dokuon.

"Think you'll pull through?"

"No."

Without another word, Tekisui got up and left.

A few days before Tekisui's own death, Keichu came from afar to ask about him. "I hear," he said to the porter, "the master's very sick."

"Yes, sir," said the porter.

"Here's a box of cakes for him. When you hand it to him, give him this message: You're old enough to die without regret." With that Keichu left.

When the porter brought the cakes to Tekisui and gave him Keichu's message, the master smiled sweetly, as if he had forgotten all pain.

23

A monk asked Master Busshin, "Do heaven and hell exist?"

"No," the master said without hesitation.

Some samurai happened to be within earshot and, amazed at Busshin's answer, asked him the same question. This time, again without hesitation, the master said, "Yes."

When accused by the samurai of being contradictory, Busshin said, "Well, if I tell *you* there's neither heaven nor hell, where would the alms come from?"

24

The Lord of Hikone, wanting to try the monk Kansan, had a beauty bathe him and treat him most tenderly.

When he had finished bathing, Kansan dismissed the girl with a smile. "Thank you," he said, "for taking so much trouble."

25

One day Tesshu, the famous swordsman and Zen devotee, went to Dokuon and told him triumphantly he believed all that exists is empty, there is no you or me, etc. The master who had listened in silence suddenly snatched up his long tobacco pipe and struck Tesshu's head.

The infuriated swordsman would have killed the master there and then, but Dokuon said calmly, "Emptiness is quick to show anger, isn't it?"

Forcing a smile, Tesshu left the room.

26

While Tokai was a visitor at a certain temple a fire started under the kitchen floor. A monk rushed into Tokai's bedroom, shouting, "A fire, master! A fire!"

"Oh?" Tokai said, sitting up. "Where?"

"Where?" exclaimed the monk. "Why, under the kitchen floor. Get up at once!"

"The kitchen, eh?" the master said drowsily. "Well, tell you what, when it reaches the passageway, come back and let me know." With this Tokai lay back and soon was snoring again.

27

Taizen, who had a good deal of Zen experience, called on the master Tetsumon (1710–   , Soto) and said, "I'm dull iron. Won't you be good enough to temper me?"

"If Peter drinks wine," said the master, "Paul will be tipsy."

"My, you're dexterous with iron."

"How's that?"

"May I offer you another cup?"

At that Tetsumon laughed heartily, and Taizen moved back three steps. "All right," said the master, "let's have some tea."

28

In his sixty-sixth year Etsugen (1616–1681, Soto) announced to his disciples on December 1, "Well, I've made up my mind to die on the eighth, the day of Buddha's awakening. If you've any questions, better ask them before then."

As the master continued to carry out all his religious duties, however, some of the monks suspected that he was having a bit of fun with them, while others were struck with grief.

On the evening of the seventh there was nothing out of the ordinary, but that night Etsugen called them all together and taught them about Sakyamuni's satori. He also entrusted his affairs to them.

At daybreak he took a bath and then, while sitting dignified in Zen, recited his last poem:

> Buddha came down from the mountain,
> I ascended it. Always I've
> Run counter to his teaching,
> And now I'm bound for hell—ha-ha!
> Man's inquisitiveness is sheer nonsense.

He then closed his eyes and, still sitting, died.

29

Master Hakugai (1343–1414, Rinzai) met a priest who was considered a wonder-worker. Among other miracles, he was supposed to be able to die and return to life at will, all in the presence of others. The master challenged him to die on the spot, and the priest attempted the trick without success.

"Buddha teaches that to try to work miracles," Hakugai admonished, "is to mislead. There's nothing strange about the Right Law, it's all perfectly clear. Heretics like you are doomed."

The repentant priest was to become Hakugai's disciple.

30

Goyu (1834–1915, Soto), when told that he would have to undergo an operation on the eye, consented at once. "We must leave such things to you doctors," he said. "Proceed."

"Good," said the doctor, "but seeing that you're rather old, we had better anesthetize."

"No need," said the master. "Get on with it."

All through the operation Goyu sat calmly, as if he were elsewhere.

31

One day Gisan, a disciplinarian, happened to see Tekisui wiping his nose with a tissue. "Fool!" he railed. "Is your nose so precious? That tissue's too good to waste on it. A virtueless man, you should know by now, is the enemy of Buddha. Just why are you pursuing Zen?"

From that moment Tekisui not only avoided wiping his nose with tissue, he took great care not to catch cold.

32

Kaishu (1807–1878, Rinzai) and his friends were crossing a raging river in heavy rain, and the boat pitched violently. All the master's friends were frightened and lost color, and some of them went so far as to invoke the aid of Avalokitesvara, the goddess of love. But Kaishu sat calmly in zazen.

When the boat made shore and his friends sighed with relief, Kaishu reprimanded them with the following: "The Zen-man is good for nothing if he can't help himself. The goddess must have laughed at your frailty."

33

When wolves were discovered in the village near Master Shoju's (1642–1721, Rinzai) temple, he entered the graveyard nightly for all of one week and sat in Zen. Strangely enough, that put a stop to the wolves' prowling. Overjoyed, the villagers asked him to describe the secret rites he had performed.

"I didn't have to resort to such things," he said, "nor could I have done so. While I was in zazen a number of wolves gathered around me, licking the tip of my nose, sniffing my windpipe. They did all sorts of silly things. But because I remained in the right state of mind, I wasn't bitten. As I keep preaching to you, the proper state of mind will make it possible for you to be free in life and death, invulnerable to fire and water. Even wolves are powerless against it. I simply tried to practice what I preach."

34

After gaining satori, Tenkei (1668–1735, Soto) went to see Master Tesshin. The master said, trying him, "I've been waiting for you a long time—what took you so long?"

"On the contrary," retorted Tenkei. "Why were you so late in seeing me?"

"My, you're talkative!"

"Try and stop me!"

Tesshin smiled and said no more.

35

While drinking tea with his disciple Tetsumon, Zen-koku (1670–1742, Soto) said, "The monk must be un-fettered in life and death."

Seeing an opportunity to begin *mondo* (Zen questioning), Tetsumon said, "What is life?"

Zenkoku held out his hands.

"What is death?"

Zenkoku joined his hands at his chest [a Chinese salutation].

"That may be your Zen," Tetsumon said, "but it isn't mine."

Now it was the master's turn. "What is life?" he said.

Tetsumon joined his hands at his chest.

"What is death?"

Tetsumon held out his hands.

"Ha!" Zenkoku said. "But you're not very firm, are you?"

Tetsumon smiled triumphantly, got to his feet, and strode out of the room.

But it was long after that Tetsumon, regretting his hauteur, realized perfect satori.

36

When Inzan (1754–1817, Rinzai) called on Gasan, the latter, before his visitor could speak a word of greeting, held out his hand and asked, "Why is this called a hand?" Then, before Inzan could reply, he stretched out a leg and said, "And why is this called a leg?"

Just as Inzan was about to answer again, Gasan clapped his hands with a laugh. The astounded monk retreated without a word. On the next day when Inzan came to the master again for instructions, Gasan cautioned him in the following way:

"These days Zen practitioners are given to trifling with the priceless koan. Without properly disciplining themselves, they are very quick to write comments or poems on the problems. They're no better than windbags, I tell you, and not one of them would make a good teacher. If you really want Zen, give up as worthless everything you've learned and experienced. Apply yourself singlemindedly. Die, then be reborn!"

Immediately after this interview, Inzan attained satori.

Anecdotes

NOTE: The half-dozen anecdotes that follow are the only items in the collection not from the Japanese masters. They are chosen from the *Hekiganroku*, a Chinese work of great antiquity composed of one hundred Zen stories with commentaries. In view of their importance to Japanese Zen, there can be no question about the appropriateness of their inclusion.

37

A heretic approached the Buddha and said, "Please tell me, O Masterful One, what is above both speech and silence?"

The Buddha made no reply.

Filled with admiration, the heretic said, "I understand, World-most-Honored. Stripped of illusion, I see at last!"

When the heretic had gone, the disciple Ananda said to the Buddha, "Hmm—I wonder what it was he saw."

"He's like a good horse," said the Buddha with a smile. "Just the shadow of the whip, and off he gallops."

38

At the death of a parishioner, Master Dogo accompanied by his disciple Zengen visited the bereaved family. Without taking the time to express a word of sympathy, Zengen went up to the coffin, rapped on it, and asked Dogo, "Is he really dead?"

"I won't say," said Dogo.

"Well?" insisted Zengen.

"I'm not saying, and that's final."

On their way back to the temple, the furious Zengen turned on Dogo and threatened, "By God, if you don't answer my question, why, I'll beat you!"

"All right, beat away."

A man of his word, Zengen slapped his master a good one.

Some time later Dogo died, and Zengen, still anxious to have his question answered, went to the master Sekiso and, after relating what had happened, asked the same question of him.

Sekiso, as if conspiring with the dead Dogo, would not answer.

"By God," cried Zengen, "you too?"

"I'm not saying, and that's final."

At that very instant Zengen experienced an awakening.

39

Butei, Emperor of Ryo, sent for Fu-daishi (*daishi*: title of honor) to explain the Diamond Sutra. On the appointed day Fu-daishi came to the palace, mounted a platform, rapped the table before him, then descended and, still not speaking, left.

Butei sat motionless for some minutes, whereupon Shiko, who had seen all that had happened, went up to him and said, "May I be so bold, sir, as to ask whether you understood?"

The Emperor sadly shook his head.

"What a pity!" Shiko exclaimed. "Fu-daishi has never been more eloquent."

40

"Other masters are always carrying on about the necessity of saving everyone," Gensha complained to his followers. "But suppose you meet up with someone deaf, dumb, and blind. He couldn't see your gestures, hear your preaching or, for that matter, ask questions. Unable to save him, you'd prove yourself a worthless Buddhist."

Troubled by these words, one of Gensha's disciples went to consult the master Unmon, who like Gensha was a disciple of Seppo.

"Bow, please," said Unmon.

The monk, though taken by surprise, obeyed the master's command, then straightened up in expectation of having his query answered. But instead of an answer he got a staff thrust at him, and he leaped back.

"Well," said Unmon, "you're not blind. Now, approach."

The monk did what he was bidden.

"Good," said Unmon. "You're not deaf either. Well, understand?"

"Understand what, sir?"

"Ah, you're not dumb either."

On hearing these words, the monk awoke as from a deep sleep.

41

A monk called on Master Bokushu and after an exchange of greetings, the master asked him where he had been living.

The monk gave out with a kwatz.

"Very good," Bokushu said, "you've treated me to a kwatz."

At this the monk gave out with another, louder than the first.

"My, you are generous," said Bokushu. "But, tell me, what happens after the third and the fourth?"

The monk, obviously confused, kept silent.

"Good-for-nothing!" Bokushu exclaimed with a hard slap to the monk's face.

42

For nearly twenty years Houn, a layman devoted to Zen, lived at Yakusan Temple and undertook discipline under Master Igen. The day came when he decided to return to his family, and the master asked ten of his disciples to see him off at the gate. It happened to be snowing and Houn, pointing up, said, "Lovely. Snowflakes beautiful as these don't fall elsewhere."

"Elsewhere?" said one of the ten. "Where is this 'elsewhere'?"

At this Houn slapped his face.

"Why did you do that, dear layman?" asked the disciple, rubbing his cheek.

"How can you pose as a Zen-man?" Houn said angrily. "You're doomed to hell!"

"And you?" the disciple cried. "What about yourself?"

Houn slapped him again. "You've eyes, but you won't see," he said over his shoulder as he moved off. "You've a mouth, but you're dumb."

INTERVIEWS WITH
MASTERS OF YAMAGUCHI

I

Yamaguchi, the "Kyoto of the West," is one of the best preserved of the castle towns of Japan, and is well known for its superb Zen temples, among them To-shun, one of the most beautiful in spite of its age (or because of it), which the billowy green of the young bamboo trees planted on the slope of the mountain against which it was built tends to belie. As has so often been the case in this crowded land, the mountain has served to protect the temple from the encroachment of those seeking breathing space on the outskirts of town. In this respect it most clearly resembles Kyoto: to its ring of mountains might be attributed the fine state of its shrines and temples, if not their very survival.

If the reader has seen Kurosawa's *Rashomon*, he will remember the opening scene: the rain, the old gate, the wasted grandeur of the temple. Well, it was raining when Takashi Ikemoto and I bicycled up from the national university where we teach, and I was strongly reminded of that scene. We parked our bicycles and entered the temple. A few minutes later we were met by Taigan Takayama, master of the Toshun, and led to his reception hall, which overlooks a lovely garden. Takayama is young (thirty-four), intellectual (a graduate in Chinese Philosophy of Kyoto University) and, Ikemoto has informed me, he journeys to Kyoto a few times a year to undergo more discipline.

Though we have had about a week to mentally prepare for the exchange, we did not think it in the spirit of Zen to prepare a list of questions. Perhaps this will turn out to be a mistake. It was agreed that we take turns asking questions and that Ikemoto would record what was said and translate the difficult parts.

Before we begin, a few words from Takayama: "I know very well that Zen is above explanation, and that the Westerner may find expository remarks in a Zen interview inadequate. Nonetheless, an exchange between a Westerner and a Japanese master might very well serve as a stimulant toward the reader's further efforts for a better appreciation of Zen. Indeed the remark that Zen is above explanation applies only to those destined to remain ignorant of it. As for those, on the other hand, possessed of insight keen enough, they will be able to intuit a Zen meaning in a master's words, spoken or written. It is my hope that the reader will read the following exchange in the proper way and, thus, see into the spirit of Zen."

STRYK: Takayama-san, as a Zen priest you have been trained in the ways of proper meditation. Now, if I were to undertake Zen discipline it would be with the view of achieving something like inner peace. Is it that which the priest seeks when meditating, or does his meditation lead him to other, more "religious" things? And if the latter is true in the case of the priest, what is it the serious lay Zen Buddhist seeks when he attempts to gain a satori awakening?

TAKAYAMA: In a sense Zen is a religion of peace of mind; therefore Zen and "inner peace" seem to be connected. But all depends on what is meant by this "inner peace," inasmuch as, complications being incidental to life, we must invariably confront them. The way of coping with them determines the nature of the "inner peace" experienced.

STRYK: You surprise me. Rightly or wrongly, I have always considered inner peace to be a rather absolute thing. If I understand correctly, you feel that the peace achieved through zazen and through satori itself is dependent on the circumstances of one's life at the time of meditation, on the things, perhaps, which made one turn to meditation in the first place. Is that right?

TAKAYAMA: Yes.

STRYK: But if a person seeks shelter in a storm, it doesn't much matter, does it, whether it is a rain or snow storm, so long as he finds on entering the shelter the protection he sought?

TAKAYAMA: This type of inner peace is different from that offered by Zen. A Zen-man, you see, must be able to keep his mental serenity in the midst of life's greatest difficulties. Here is a well-known Zen poem by Manura, the Twenty-second Patriarch of India:

> The mind moveth with the ten thousand things:
> Even when moving, it is serene.
> Perceive its essence as it moveth on,
> And neither joy nor sorrow there is.

(translated by D. T. Suzuki)

This "being serene" is the inner peace of Zen. As to your second question, of course both priest and layman seek the selfsame serenity.

IKEMOTO: When recently questioned about the secret of manipulating his puppets, a prominent American artist replied: "The most important thing is to love the puppets. When I manipulate Judy, my fingers become Judy. When I move the monkey, they become the monkey. I forget myself and become the thing I handle. That's the secret." Now, it seems to me that his words resemble those of a Zen master. Am I right in thinking that the puppeteer has realized a Zen state, at least as far as his art is concerned?

TAKAYAMA: Perfectly right.

STRYK: I dislike leaving that puppeteer, but there is something that interests me very much. Ikemoto-san has pointed out to me that unlike Christian mystics who seek vision, the Zen-man seeks release from vision. It is sometimes described, is it not, as a vision of emptiness? Now, is this image of nothingness complete and instantaneous or, to use the metaphor of the room, does one cushion at a time, say, then the walls themselves, have to be removed?

TAKAYAMA: I'm very much afraid that Zen has nothing to do with your vision of nothingness. How can one have such a vision?

STRYK: Well, we've all tried to vision the reaches of space, haven't we? Surely the open eye *sees*, even emptiness.

TAKAYAMA: Nevertheless Zen, which disowns all that has form, rejects any and all kinds of vision. According to it, a mountain is not high, nor is a pillar vertical. Emptiness in Zen is that in which being and non-being originate. It is realized, if you continue to insist on the term, when the dualism of being and non-being is done away with. The emptiness is not there as something to be seen or not seen, it is what you have become. And its realization is instantaneous, meaning timeless, without beginning or end. It is perhaps to be conceded that one can experience emptiness at a given moment, but the experience itself transcends time.

IKEMOTO: While we're on the subject of that experience, Dr. Daisetsu Suzuki, who as you know is a follower of the Rinzai sect, has always been of the opinion that there is no Zen without satori. It appears that Western readers of Dr. Suzuki have been intrigued above all by his dramatic descriptions of satori awakening. Yet the Soto sect, which has many more adherents, insists on the primacy of sitting in meditation without seeking satori. With Westerners in mind, what is your opinion of the Soto standpoint?

TAKAYAMA: Simply though perhaps inadequately put, it seems that Rinzai Zen is more accessible to Westerners.

STRYK: To continue our discussion of satori, exactly what does one feel as distinct from what one sees, or no longer sees, at the moment of the awakening, and how long does the feeling last?

TAKAYAMA: The feeling will differ with individuals, of course, but perhaps I can say this much. Until the coming of satori one's being is filled with doubt. At the moment of awakening the Zen-man is beside himself with joy to know that he has discovered THAT properly. This ecstasy will not last very long, maybe only a few hours, but after satori he cannot move outside its world whether awake or asleep. As you well know, Zen masters are in the habit of expressing in verse their state of mind while in satori. The following poem by Yomyo-Enju, a Chinese master, is among the best known. It may be helpful to know that he had his awakening at the instant of hearing a pile of firewood topple.

> Toppling over is none other than THAT:
> Nowhere is found an atom of dust.
> Mountains, rivers, plain—
> All reveal the Buddha-body.

Satori will make it possible for you to live constantly in a state of joy. But remember that one needs further discipline to rid oneself of this joy, for there must not be even the shadow of attachment, any kind of attachment, in Zen. In this way you can attain a genuine awakening.

IKEMOTO (after tea and a few minutes of small talk): In principle, Zen masters should be able to read and utilize any kind of writing. Again with Westerners in mind, do you think that even the Bible could be read and commented on from the Zen point of view?

TAKAYAMA: Why not? If, that is, a talented master sets about it.

STRYK: Since Ikemoto-san brought up Westerners again, in a recent article read by each of us the writer states that unlike Westerners, Japanese are Zen-minded, and for that reason Zen as it is practiced here is really inaccessible to someone like myself. Do you agree? To pursue this in a different way, were you more Zen-minded than your friends at the university? Would many of them have been able to undergo Zen training? And here I am perhaps repeating myself: would a serious Westerner have a fair chance of understanding Zen, finding the true path? And if so, why do some Westerners known for their interest in Zen speak of the effectiveness of certain drugs in the attainment of satori? Is drug taking compatible with Zen practice in Japan?

TAKAYAMA: I'll take these questions up one by one. It is true, perhaps, that Zen may be somewhat inaccessible to Westerners. This is only natural. Of course in itself, as you fully realize, Zen has no such limitations: there's no East nor West in it. But in its most important manifestations it has been characterized by geographical and historical features peculiar to China and Japan. Indeed it may very well be these special features which most strongly appeal to the West. And maybe for that very reason, I should add, they stand more or less in the way of a Westerner's attainment of real insight, let alone Zen awakening. Speaking of myself, I was not more Zen-minded than my fellow students in Kyoto, and I firmly believe that anyone should be able to profit by Zen discipline, though it is undeniable that some people, by reason of character and temperament, are more suited to the discipline than others. If a Westerner can find a master willing to train him, he should be able to find the true path you speak of as quickly as a Japanese, always assuming of course that he understands the language. As you are no doubt aware, history offers many such instances. When Zen thrived in China, a number of Japanese went there to study and some of them attained true satori. It should be unnecessary to add that they already had before leaving these shores a proper knowledge of Chinese culture in particular and Buddhism in general to make the experience profitable. Finally, and most emphatically, drug taking is not compatible with Zen.

IKEMOTO: Both of us are teachers of literature and are interested in Zen poetry. As you probably know, the contemporary poet Shinkichi Takahashi has undergone regular discipline and, it seems, is known as a Zen poet among his fellow writers. What do you think of the following poem, one of his most recent?

The Peach

A little girl under a peach tree,
Whose blossoms fall into the entrails
Of the earth.

There you stand, but a mountain may be there
Instead; it is not unlikely that the earth
May be yourself.

You step against a plate of iron and half
Your face is turned to iron. I will smash
Flesh and bone

And suck the cracked peach. She went up the mountain
To hide her breasts in the snowy ravine.
Women's legs

Are more or less alike. The leaves of the peach tree
Stretch across the sea to the end of
The continent.

The sea was at the little girl's beck and call.
I will cross the sea like a hairy
Caterpillar

And catch the odor of your body.

TAKAYAMA: Most interesting, from both the Zen and
the literary points of view. Let's begin with the former:
an Avatamsaka doctrine holds that the universe can be
observed from the four angles of (1) phenomena, (2)
noumenon, (3) the identity of noumenon and phenomena, and (4) the mutual identity of phenomena.
Now, whether he was aware of it or not, the poet de-
picted a world in which noumenon and phenomena are
identical. Considering the poem with Zen in mind, the
lesson to be drawn, I suppose, is that one should not
loiter on the way but proceed straight to one's destination—the viewpoint of the mutual identity of phenomena. But from a literary point of view, the significance,
and the charm of the poem lies in its metaphorical pre-

sentation of a world in which noumenon and phenomena are identified with each other.

STRYK: A very profound reading. I must confess that I didn't see half as much in the poem, though I like it very much for the freedom of imagination and the harshness of tone. To continue with the arts, do you think Zen could be "used" by artists, as might have been the case with the master-painter Sesshu, to achieve, well, the proper state of mind for serious production?

TAKAYAMA: Zen is not something to be "used." Its art is nothing more than an expression of Zen spirit.

STRYK: I see. Well then, how would you describe that spirit, as it relates, that is, to the artist and his work? And though here I may be asking too much, would you say that artists—painters, writers, composers—might gain by periods of discipline? And if so, what have they to gain that drink or, to be more consistent, prayer and the seeking of vision might not be able to afford with far less difficulty? Finally have you yourself felt, however vaguely, creative while meditating? I ask because I have always thought of creative activity as being an assertion of self, and can't imagine its taking place in a state of "non-being."

TAKAYAMA: In a sense I have already described the Zen spirit or state of mind. Doubtless there are artists who try to achieve through Zen the proper spirit for serious production. Well, I'll try to relate the Zen mind to the artist and his work, though I should mention at once that I myself am not an artist and, to answer one of your questions, have not felt even vaguely creative while meditating. Let's put it this way: it is a state of mind in which one is identified with an object without any sense of restraint. In this connection one could mention the wakefulness of Zuigan, the Chinese master, who had the following dialogue with himself every day:

Master!
Yes, sir!
Be wide awake!
Yes, sir!
And from now on don't let anyone deceive you!
Yes, sir! Yes, sir!

When an artist, in this state of mind, depicts an object in words, he has a fine poem; when in lines, a true picture. Fundamentally, however, Zen offers nothing to gain, but there is something in this non-gaining which quite naturally becomes part of the Zen-man's whole being. As Rinzai, the founder of our sect, put it, you gain worthiness without seeking it. No, after all, I suppose it is possible to say that artists would gain by Zen. As to what it offers the artist who seeks inspiration from it that drink, say, cannot hope to give him, well, try it and see.

STRYK: You tempt me, but I'm sure to find the discipline too strict. By the way, have you yourself ever found it to be too strict? I ask this from a rather special point of view, from that of one who might find it too difficult, even impossible, to accept discipleship in an order so authoritarian but who is very willing to concede that the authority must be imposed for the good of the initiate.

TAKAYAMA: No, I have never felt the discipline to be too strict. Indeed it is a very tough mental job at times, especially during a period of *sesshin* when for seven days, all day long, one is trained in devotional matters. But I am simply grateful for all this.

STRYK: Our time is almost up and Ikemoto-san, out of his usual courtesy, insists that I ask the final questions. You have heard of the great interest in Zen in my country. I understand that while in Kyoto you were sometimes approached by Americans seeking explanations. From your reading and observation, do you think it likely that those Americans who think of themselves as Zen-men, and there are a fair number, know what true Zen is? Is not the taking of drugs, upon which you have already commented, a simple confession of defeat? And what about those who think that satori or something like it can be gained through drink or strenuous love-making? Last of all, does Zen have anything to offer the serious Westerner who, though he may not wish to undergo discipline, feels himself in search of a truer way?

TAKAYAMA: Well, I would have to meet those Americans you speak of before passing judgment. But, yes, drug taking as it relates to the seeking of an awakening, could very well be described as a confession of defeat. By the same token, those given to excessive drinking and woman chasing and who still hope for Zen are no doubt deluding themselves. Certainly they have never heard the old Zen saying: "A man of consummate activity knows no rules to follow." Zen offers Something to everyone, Westerner or Oriental, but just what it offers is beyond conceptual understanding. Indeed Zen is always offering that Something, and offering it directly. People just can't seem to grasp it.

147

II

The Joei Temple in Yamaguchi City is known throughout Japan for the rock garden laid behind it by Sesshu (1420–1506), Zen master and one of the greatest painters in the Chinese style. The garden has been lovingly preserved by generations of Zen priests who doubtless were chosen to serve at Joei for their personal qualities. Yasuda-Tenzan-Roshi, the present master of Joei, possesses such qualities. He is very well known, even revered, in Yamaguchi as an expert in the art of tea and one who is familiar with the other arts historically associated with Zen.

From all over Japan people converge on Joei Temple, usually on Sundays and often in large tour groups. But on weekdays it is possible to feel isolated there, and apart from the pleasant sound of ducks paddling in the garden pond and, alas, the occasional blare of a loudspeaker giving a description of the garden when such is requested, there is silence.

The garden lies at the foot of one of the many fair-sized mountains circling the city, and the impression made on the visitor is that of a perfect unity of art and nature, a Zen ideal. One is at a loss to define where the garden ends and the mountain slope begins, so well did Sesshu's genius achieve this desired unity. The mountain is thick with pine and bamboo, through which a path winds from the garden, and at times the whole appears to be one gigantic various tree. Wandering up the path alone, one may find oneself having some rather strange bird-like illusions.

It is autumn, the most beautiful season in Yama-guchi, and Takashi Ikemoto and I are looking forward to the exchange on Zen with the roshi. The appointed day is a fine one, and though as in the case of our first interview with a master we haven't prepared questions, we feel confident that the meeting will be a fruitful one. We bicycle out to Joei and are met at the gate by the roshi himself. Our greetings are very informal, and the roshi leads us to a room with a fine view of the garden, which I have grown to love, and immediately begins preparing green tea on a brazier. It has been decided that this time, in the interest of consistency, we ask our questions separately (if I know him as well as I think, Ikemoto-san will insist that I ask most of them). At his insistence I begin.

STRYK: Roshi, it is very good of you to take the time to answer our questions, but please, if you find any of them too sensitive, say so.

ROSHI: Open mindedness, I like to feel, is character-istic of Zen masters, especially when you compare them with those of other Buddhist sects. I've nothing to hide, though of course I can't promise to answer questions that are too personal.

STRYK: I have heard that *wabi* (the spirit of poverty and self-denial) is rarely to be found in modern tea ceremonies, and that most people attend them to show off their finery. As a well-known tea master you are in a position to know; is this true? We know that everything in modern society would tend to make a mockery of seeking *wabi*. Is the tea ceremony as it was originally performed by masters like Rikyu (1521–1591) doomed because of this?

Roshi: I agree with what you say about wabi. You find all too little of it in tea ceremonies these days, something I'm always complaining about to those who attend the monthly ceremonies here. But you must bear in mind that though wabi is a state of scarcity, it doesn't mean lacking in things. Rather they should be cast aside, or at least not used, nor even seen, during the ceremony; the ideal is to minimize life's essentials. Suppose you live in a mansion. You should have tea in a room of four-and-a-half mats or less. After all, the spirit of tea is the spirit of Zen itself, and can be described with the words simplicity, conciseness, intuition. I'm afraid that ceremonies today are like those in the feudal castles before Rikyu's time. People prize, as they did then, expensive utensils and what not. It was from the time of the master Enshu (1579–1647) that the cult began to introduce artistic elements. Needless to say, in the old days women did not take part in the ceremonies. Nowadays the ceremony is not serious enough for my taste. It's like a social gathering, a recreation for well-to-do women. Yes, I feel with you that tea as conceived by masters like Rikyu may be doomed, though, I hasten to add, there will always be a core of traditionalists.

Stryk: While we're on the subject of tea and Rikyu, in reading accounts of his last ceremony with his inmates, at the end of which he was on Lord Hideyoshi's order to commit suicide, I have been disturbed by a few of the things that are supposed to have happened. You'll recall that after breaking the cup with the words, "Never again shall this cup, polluted by the lips of misfortune, be used by man," and then dismissing his friends save for the most intimate of them all, he killed himself "with a smile on his face." Now, it seems to me that the breaking of the cup and his expression of self-sorrow, however justified in the human sense, were neither in keeping with the spirit of tea nor the famous stoicism of Zen. When we compare Rikyu with Socrates, who died by poisoning himself in almost exactly the same circumstances, Zen does not come out as well as Greek stoicism. Have you yourself ever been disturbed by what I have sensed to be an inconsistency in Rikyu's final act?

Roshi: I'm not certain that the breaking of the cup is a historical fact, but if it is a comment must be made. First of all, you must understand that Rikyu, though a great tea master, was very far from attaining perfect Zen, which is clearly revealed in his death poem, a most unsatisfactory one from the Zen standpoint. Take for example the line, "I kill both Buddhas and Patriarchs." I'm afraid that contains very little Zen, and it shows that he failed to reach the state of an "old gimlet," or mature Zen-man, one whose "point" has been blunted by long use. The Zen title "Rikyu" had been given him by his teacher Kokei in the hope that it might help him soften his temper, but all that was in vain. Kokei once praised Rikyu in a poem, speaking of him as "an old layman immersed in Zen for thirty years," yet one can surmise, Rikyu was unable to discipline himself through use of the koan. Incidentally, as you probably know, it was Sotan, Rikyu's grandson, who created the wabi tea cult. Sotan had taken a regular course of Zen study. From what I've said, I hope you see that Rikyu was not a true Zen-man and for that reason cannot be compared, at least as a representative of Zen, with a great sage like Socrates.

Stryk: That's most interesting. Now, if you'll permit me to change the subject and ask one of those sensitive questions I threatened you with, I'd like to begin by saying that I'm troubled by two seemingly minor things in contemporary Japanese culture, as it relates to temples, gardens and monuments. And, if you don't mind my saying so, both are to be encountered right here at the Joei.

ROSHI: Don't hesitate to ask your questions.

STRYK: Thank you. Well, the first concerns the use of that loudspeaker out there. I realize that it is used to inform visitors of the very interesting history of your temple and Sesshu's garden, and that loudspeakers are used in exactly the same way at all the famous places in Japan, yet because of the blaring it's not really possible to feel the calm which, among other things, one comes to find. As loudspeakers serve merely an educational end, could not printed information suffice? The other, more important thing I have in mind is the apparent need to supply obvious "comparisons" for visitors. In Akiyoshi Cave we are informed that certain formations resemble mushrooms, others rice paddies, etc. Here at your temple some of the garden rocks out there are supposed to look like mountains in China, and of course both Akiyoshi Cave and Sesshu's garden have their Mount Fujis. Even the world-famous Ryoanji rock garden in Kyoto is spoken of in this way. It all amounts to an aesthetic sin, I'm inclined to feel, and I use a word as strong as that because such naïve analogizing runs strongly counter to the genius of Japanese art which, most would agree, consists of great subtlety and suggestiveness, as in Basho's poetry. Finally isn't it true that Zen, being very direct in all matters, would insist that a rock is a rock? I have it on good authority that masters like Sesshu did not themselves make these curious comparisons. Why not leave it to the visitor to imagine for himself, if he is so inclined, what such things look like?

ROSHI: Fundamentally no information about the garden is necessary, I suppose, but really, you know, in order to appreciate his garden fully you must have almost as much insight as Sesshu himself. This, needless to say, very few possess. Ideally one should sit in Zen for a long period before looking at the garden; then one might be able to look at it, as the old saying goes, "with the navel." But to answer your questions, one at a time. As things stand I'm obliged to resort to such devices as the loudspeaker, especially when a large, hurried group of tourists comes, because, frankly, most of them would scarcely bother to read printed information. The "blaring" you hear out there, unpleasant as it may be, serves an end, you see. After all, it's important to me at least that as many people as possible are informed of the essentials of Sesshu's gardening. Next, the problem of supplying "comparisons." Sesshu, it is true, left no written record of this type. The description of the garden given today seems to have started in the Meiji era (1867–1912). Nevertheless it's most important to keep certain things clear. Sesshu was the first Japanese painter to adopt the technique of sketching, which in his hands became something like abstract painting. As the Zen method of expresson is symbolic, it is likely that Mount Fuji out there (and you'll have to admit that the rock does look like it) represents Japan, while some of the other mountain-rocks represent China, and so on. In other words the garden is an embodiment of the universe, as seen by a Zen master. In short, those are symbols you see out there, not naïve resemblances.

STRYK: I understand, but perhaps what I have in mind is the tendency itself. For example, last Sunday I visited a Zen temple in Ube, and the priest was good enough to take me around the back for a look at the garden. A very beautiful one, I should add. Well, without even being asked he began pointing to the rocks and shrubbery and offering comparisons. As the garden is laid on a slope, it appears that the azalea bushes which fringe the foot of the slope (they're not in bloom now, of course) represent clouds. Frankly I wish he had simply permitted me to take a look at the garden. But perhaps we've spoken enough about the few things that have troubled me, and I must say that you have answered my questions about them with the greatest forbearance. Something I saw inside the temple at Ube leads me to my next question. A group of men were sitting inside having tea, and when I asked the priest about them I was informed that they had come to consult him about the traditional Zen-sitting for laymen, which, I understand, usually takes place twice a year, at the hottest and coldest times. These men formed a very mixed group, it seemed to me, and I've heard that those who come to temples for zazen represent all walks of life. Is that right? What is it they seek? Are they troubled? Do any of them succeed in attaining satori? Do you preach to them in a special way? As you see it, is the zazen session as necessary in these days of psychoanalysis and so forth, as it was in the past? What, in short, has the layman to gain by lodging in a cold Zen temple, eating only rice and vegetables, and while sitting in Zen, being whacked if he so much as dozes? Finally among those who come to your temple for the sessions are there some who work, in one way or another, in the arts?

Roshi: Most of the people who come here are students who, for the most part, are merely restless. They want *hara* (abdomen, or Zen, composure). Then there are the neurotics who come accompanied by their protectors, and older people who are troubled in one way or another. Many come simply for the calm, others, university lecturers, for example, because they are not able to find as much in other religions. I'm afraid that very few of them, whatever their reason for coming, attain satori worthy of the name. They may or may not be given a koan, but after all one's problem can be koan enough. I give a *teisho* (lecture on a Zen text) on such books as *Mumonkan* or *Hekiganroku*. Additionally, and this is a feature of the Rinzai sect, there is dokusan, or individual guidance. Whether the session ends in success or not depends on the temperaments of the participants and on the efforts they make. On a slightly different subject, perhaps you know that Professor Kasamatsu of Tokyo University has conducted experiments, through measuring brain waves, on a Zen priest engaged in zazen. He's found that even those who've been sitting for as long as twenty years do not have "tranquilized" brain waves. But I seriously doubt the importance of such experiments. As to whether those who come here for zazen are in any way connected with the arts, I suspect so, but really we don't go into such things.

STRYK: You are aware of the great interest in Zen in the West. Some feel that it is due to the same needs that made Existentialism and phenomenological thinking so popular in the years following World War II. Briefly this might have been due to a kind of enlightenment, a sudden need for simplicity, directness, and the formation of a world of real things and manageable experiences. In other words, the disillusionment with high-sounding phrases, idealistic concepts, and intellectualism generally, forced men to search out something radically different. In some measure Zen seems to offer an adequate substitute for the unrealizable promises of idealism. Is this your feeling too? Finally do you think that, given the major reasons for the need of so great a change in the way men view living, as far as the West is concerned, Zen can, among other things, teach us how to achieve peace?

Roshi: It appears that the great interest in Zen in the West is motivated by utilitarianism. This may be good or bad, but it's important to bear in mind that Zen does not aim directly at simplicity. The Zen-man's chief aim is to gain satori, to which simplicity, directness, and so forth, are mere adjuncts. Indeed it is quite impossible that there be an awakening without such mental tendencies. In this respect, I gather, Zen seems to be able to satisfy the new spiritual needs of the West. Really, you know, in one sense Zen is the only religion capable of helping the world achieve peace. Its fundamental teaching is that all things are Buddhas—not men alone but all things, sentient and non-sentient. And not merely the earth, but the other planets as well. Universal peace will be realized when men all over the world bow to the preciousness and sacredness of everything. Zen, which teaches them to do this, is the religion of the Space Age.

Stryk: My final question deals with the arts and touches on Sesshu and your temple. What would you say are the chief qualities of Zen art, be it painting, poetry, drama, or gardening. To put the question in another way, and to narrow it considerably, when you look at a scroll by Sesshu, when you look out at this marvelous garden, in what way do you feel his creations to be different from those works of Japanese art which, though perhaps equally important, have no connection with Zen? Last of all, what is there about Western art, if anything, that might leave you as a Zen master dissatisfied?

ROSHI (returning from a back room with an album of Sesshu reproductions): What expresses cosmic truth in the most direct and concise way—that is the heart of Zen art. Please examine this picture, "Fisherman and Woodcutter." Of all Sesshu's pictures, this is my favorite. The boat at the fisherman's back tells us his occupation, the bundle of firewood behind the woodcutter tells his. The fisherman is drawn with only three strokes of the brush, the woodcutter with five. You couldn't ask for greater concision. And these two men, what are they talking about? In all probability, and this the atmosphere of the picture suggests, they are discussing something very important, something beneath the surface of daily life. How do I know? Why, every one of Sesshu's brush strokes tells me. I'm sorry to say that I'm not very familiar with Western art, though occasionally I'll drop in to see an exhibition. To be sure, Western art has volume and richness when it is good. Yet to me it is too thickly encumbered by what is dispensable. It's as if the Western artist were trying to hide something, not reveal it.

STRYK: Thank you for answering my questions so frankly and thoughtfully. Now it's Ikemoto-san's turn.

IKEMOTO: Thank you. My questions will be of a more personal nature. To my knowledge, Roshi, you are the only qualified master in this prefecture. Please tell us about your career from the beginning.

ROSHI: I was born of peasant parents and went to

live in a temple in my sixth year. In those days it was customary for one of the children of a religious family to enter the priesthood, and an uncle of mine was a Zen priest. I began to study Zen in the second year of Junior High School, but it was only after the university that I underwent serious training. The temples I chose for this purpose were Tofukuji, Bairinji, Yogenji, and Engakuji, which are located in different parts of the country. I obtained my Zen testimonial from Ienaga-Ichido-Roshi, chief abbot of Tofukuji. I learned from him how to handle koans in the way favored by the Takuju school of the Rinzai sect, but I also desired to know how to deal with koans according to methods used by the Inzan school of the same sect (it seems a pity to me that few students of Rinzai Zen nowadays desire to know about both schools), so I went to Engakuji in Kamakura. There under the master Furukawa-Gyodo-Roshi I succeeded in my purpose. His strictness impressed me. His own teacher, by the way, was the famous Shaku-Soen-Roshi, one of whose lay disciples is Dr. D. T. Suzuki of Western fame. Soen-Roshi, a scholarly master, was very different from Gyodo-Roshi, of course, but both were great masters.

IKEMOTO: Could you tell us how and under what circumstances you achieved satori? I ask you to do this because reading an account of your experience may encourage students of Zen.

ROSHI (his face brightening): It happened on the fifth day of the special December training at Yogenji, while I was engaged in what is called night-sitting. As is sometimes done, a few of us left the meditation hall and, choosing a spot in the deep snow near the river, began our Zen-sitting, each of us engrossed in his koan. I was not conscious of time, nor did I feel the cold.

Suddenly the temple bell struck the second hour, time of the first morning service, which we were expected to attend. I tried to get up, but my feet were so numb with cold that I fell to the snow. At that very instant it happened, my satori. It was an enrapturing experience, one I could not hope to describe adequately. This was my first satori; now about my second. But you may be wondering why more than one satori?

IKEMOTO: I understand that it often happens to true Zen-men.

ROSHI: It was the second satori, experienced at En-gakuji, that gave me complete freedom of thought and action. As I've already said, Gyodo-Roshi valued activity above all else. He gave me Joshu's Mu as koan. Well, for a whole year every view of it I offered was curtly rejected by the master. But this was the Inzan method of dealing with the koan. At any rate, one day on my way back from *sanzen* (presenting one's view of a koan to the master) and while descending the temple steps, I tripped and fell. As I fell I had my second satori, a consummate one. I owe a great deal to Gyodo-Roshi, for without his guidance I might have ended up a mere adherent of koans, a man without insight into his true nature, which is afforded only by an awakening.

IKEMOTO: Most interesting, Roshi. By the way, this is the so-called "instant age." I wish there were a special recipe for gaining satori instantly.

ROSHI: Well, the master Ishiguro-Horyu is said to have devised a way of training toward that end. It's rather easy to get Zen students to have special experiences, such as hearing the sound of falling incense ash or feeling themselves afloat. But that's not satori. Satori consists of a return to one's ordinary self, if you know what I mean—the most difficult thing in the world.

IKEMOTO: I understand. Finally may I ask whether you are training successors?

ROSHI: A Zen master is duty-bound to transmit the nearly untransmittable truth to at least one successor. But everything depends on circumstances. You see, it's not a matter of five or six years. A training period of fifteen to twenty years is necessary. I am awaiting the appearance of earnest seekers after the truth.

ANCHOR BOOKS

BRITISH FICTION

CONRAD, JOSEPH The Secret Agent, A8
—— The Shadow-Line, Typhoon *and* The Secret Sharer, A178
—— Under Western Eyes, ed. Zabel, A323
—— Victory, A106
—— Youth, Heart of Darkness *and* The End of the Tether, A173
KIPLING, RUDYARD The English in England: Short Stories by Rudyard Kipling, ed. Jarrell, A362
—— In the Vernacular: The English in India, ed. Jarrell, A363
MISH, CHARLES C., ed. Anchor Anthology of Short Fiction of the Seventeenth Century, AC1
SNOW, C. P. The Masters, A162
WEINTRAUB, STANLEY, ed. The Yellow Book: Quintessence of the Nineties, A421

CONTINENTAL FICTION

ALAIN-FOURNIER, HENRI The Wanderer, A14
CHEKHOV, ANTON Ward No. 6 *Six Russian Short Novels,* ed. Jarrell, A348
COLETTE My Mother's House *and* The Vagabond, A62
DOSTOEVSKY Three Short Novels of Dostoevsky, A193
FLORES, ANGEL, ed. Nineteenth Century German Tales, A184
GOGOL, NIKOLAI The Overcoat *Six Russian Short Novels,* ed. Jarrell, A348
JARRELL, RANDALL, ed. Six Russian Short Novels, A348
LERMONTOV, MIHAIL A Hero of Our Time, A133
LESKOV, NIKOLAI The Lady Macbeth of the Mtsensk District *Six Russian Short Novels,* ed. Jarrell, A348
MERWIN, W. S., trans. The Life of Lazarillo de Tormes, A316
SERGE, VICTOR The Case of Comrade Tulayev, A349
TOLSTOY, LEO The Death of Ivan Ilych *and* Master and Man *Six Russian Short Novels,* ed. Jarrell, A348
TURGENEV, IVAN A Lear of the Steppes *Six Russian Short Novels,* ed. Jarrell, A348

ORIENTAL LITERATURE

KAI-YU, HSU, trans. & ed. Twentieth Century Chinese Poetry—An Anthology, A413
KANG-HU, KIANG The Jade Mountain—Being Three Hundred Poems of the T'ang Dynasty 618–906, trans. Bynner, A411
MURASAKI, LADY The Tale of Genji, trans. Waley Vol. I—A55
SCOTT, A. C. Literature and the Arts in Twentieth Century China, A343
TSAO HSUEH-CHIN Dream of the Red Chamber, trans. Wang, A159

ANCHOR BOOKS

POETRY

APOLLINAIRE, GUILLAUME Alcools: Poems 1898–1913, trans. Meredith, A444

AUDEN, W. H., KALLMAN, CHESTER, & GREENBERG, NOAH, eds. An Elizabethan Song Book, A56

BLACKMUR, R. P. Form and Value in Modern Poetry, A96

BLOOM, HAROLD, ed. English Romantic Poetry, Vol. I: Blake, Wordsworth, Coleridge & others, A347a

—— English Romantic Poetry, Vol. II: Byron, Shelley, Keats & others, A347b

CHAUCER, GEOFFREY The Canterbury Tales of Geoffrey Chaucer, ed. Cook, A265

CRANE, HART The Complete Poems of Hart Crane, ed. Frank, A128

DEUTSCH, BABETTE Poetry in Our Time, A344

DICKINSON, EMILY Selected Poems and Letters of Emily Dickinson, ed. Linscott, A192

FITZGERALD, ROBERT, trans. The Odyssey, A333

FLORES, ANGEL, ed. An Anthology of French Poetry, A134

—— An Anthology of Spanish Poetry, A268

GOETHE Goethe's Faust, trans. Kaufmann, A328

GRAVES, ROBERT The Poems of Robert Graves, A139

HENDERSON, HAROLD G. An Introduction to Haiku, A150

HOFFMAN, DANIEL, ed. American Poetry and Poetics, A304

HOMER The Odyssey, trans. Fitzgerald, A333

KAI-YU, HSU, trans. & ed. Twentieth Century Chinese Poetry—An Anthology, A413

KANG-HU, KIANG The Jade Mountain—Being Three Hundred Poems of the T'ang Dynasty 618–906, trans. Bynner, A411

KAUFMANN, WALTER, trans. Goethe's Faust, A328

KELLY, ROBERT & LEARY, PARIS, eds. A Controversy of Poets, A439

KIPLING, RUDYARD A Choice of Kipling's Verse, ed. Eliot, A301

MELVILLE, HERMAN Selected Poems of Herman Melville, ed. Cohen, A375

MILLER, PERRY, ed. The American Puritans, A80

——, trans. & ed. The Ring of Words—An Anthology of Song Texts, A428

SANTAYANA, GEORGE Three Philosophical Poets: Lucretius, Dante, Goethe, A17

SAPPHO Lyrics in the Original Greek with Translations by Willis Barnstone, A400

SIDNEY, SIR PHILIP The Psalms of Sir Philip Sidney and the Countess of Pembroke, ed. Rathmell, A311

TERRY, PATRICIA, trans. The Lays of Courtly Love, A369

VAUGHAN, HENRY The Complete Poetry of Henry Vaughan, ed. Fogle, AC7

VIRGIL The Aeneid of Virgil, trans. Lewis, A20

—— The Eclogues and Georgics of Virgil. In the Original Latin with a Verse Translation by C. Day Lewis, A390

WILLIAMS, JOHN, ed. English Renaissance Poetry: A Collection of Shorter Poems from Skelton to Jonson, A359